# Bloodlines

by
Christopher Alexander Berg

CCB Publishing
British Columbia, Canada

Bloodlines

Copyright ©2018 by Christopher Alexander Berg
ISBN-13   978-1-77143-352-5
First Edition

Library and Archives Canada Cataloguing in Publication
Berg, Christopher Alexander, 1978-, author
Bloodlines / by Christopher Alexander Berg -- First edition.
Poems.
ISBN 978-1-77143-352-5 (pbk.).
Additional cataloguing data available from Library and Archives Canada

Cover artwork design by: Christopher Alexander Berg

Publisher:     CCB Publishing
               British Columbia, Canada
               www.ccbpublishing.com

Here at the ninth gate

The light paints

darkness... seeking black

Those in back...

you're up now

All is stacked
to crash down

upon us...

We're all just
kids
brainwashed

Unfit to live

Names lost, ashore

Sons of whores
we are
(Blood on thorns)

*Bloodlines*

Bring me the heads of stardom

Postpartum... depression

affecting God

Rejecting all

these days

Neglecting all

No one's here who's anyone

said the gun

pointed at
everyone

(off safety)

Don't hate me
cause I'm beautiful

just hate me

Through shame we
walk ... unashamed

Entertained

by stage names

pushing change

When the world rots,

you'll thank me

Insane we,

haven't killed it yet

We think it's real...

but they're playing Atari

Dollar bill roles

starring the starving

(We're all famous now)

selling these heartbeats

to all running crowds

(dodging their offspring)

Candles on the carpet...

lit...

Spit...

flying with shots... drops

of blood..., drip

Lips...

can't sense
their last kiss

Clips... round trip

make the population dip

Why must there be... a hell?

People are poison...

joining... up

with all that's
destroying

us...

Employing... us

voices

(hoping we'll listen)

(hoping we'll give in...

to all temptations around us)

The ground just

said it's last goodbyes


Only half the sun came 'round
today

The other half...

pretended to be the moon

(crescent shaped)

Anal gaped...

teens...

don't need a face

(Eater of dreams...,

we are...

pyramid schemes)


The trees aren't growing, they're reaching,
not standing, but leaving... the "woulds" of this world...
for the "shoulds" of the grieving.

A moment I'll take now...

to stand for
the fall down.

Opponents...,
just for
condolence...

needing a hand.

The last man

on earth
will wish he was the first

to die...

Black ties...,

only on the buried

past lives...

that were never carried

... to safety

To say we...

deserve another chance,

is crazy

Today we...

may become the ants


I forgot till I remembered...

transgendered

queens

tell me your dreams

(as long as they aren't of love)

Some...
people
just...
won't open...

Most in ... fact are boneless
roaches

poaching for a presence


Tell me the price of present... day's

dreaded stay...

"I'm wondering if what to wear...,

just in case the world ends."

How do we
get back
to normal?

Can we?

Hijacked and ransacked...,

our morals.

(Damning)

Is there a home for us?

... A place left?

In the future our bones
will rust...

... created ...

(Inhuman)

In nooses...,

we'll hang for "equal rights"

Christmas lights

flashing...

Twisted minds

passing...

knowledge to
sickened mimes

Missing lines...

"What are they?"

Live in 5...

and can't say...

anything truthful.

Brutal...,

people in every walk

At fault

for quakes
and after shocks

"Send in the titans."


We're patches
of scratches
on matches
in batches
with hatchets
and magic
subtracting
attraction

Invading
what's fading
still waiting
for saving
defaming
the changing
embracing
defacing

Appointed
are noises
disjointed
with choices
exploited
and poisoned
They're voices
avoided

Resentment
revisits
incentives
with visions
Repentance
resisted
committed
fictitious


Heads or tails ... to save yourselves...,

... for me to kill later

Engraved your
name within
the madness

Practice
what you preach
or vanish

Vantage... points on all the stranded,

sanded ... souls with edges banished

"Calling on all with conscience."

Consequence...,

shunning

dominance

Cumming...,

on many fresh faces we are

"We're far...

enough along the way

right now."

Lunatic high

grooving in
zoom again

Crucifix time...

Innocence
irrelevant

New in this lie?

Remember
the bitter

Shooting at signs...

proving...,
undoings

Purple rain, hurled...

purple shame

My name?

(unimportant)

It's divorced from

me...

On course to bleed,

we are

all sorts of things

"The next election will be our last."

Mass...,

shootings ... (a popular

hashtag)

Gift bags?

"No."

A gift that's
loaned...,

life.

"But too much just doesn't seem right."

Sleep tight? Do I?

"No."

My eyes ... closed

see more

See war...

See hell in many forms

(All here...

in fashion)

large factions

of death ... coming

(request something)

Hard actions...

lives passing

away at high rates

The dates are not safe

"Happy death day."

Time to get away (right now)


Hacking into the control room

(I'm here)

Tapping in ... a force field

Napping in ... a coarse sealed ... up

(Wondering which way to go)

Making my own luck...

Your foam guts,

I hate

In no shape..., we are

today...

"I think we're gonna die soon."

Call it faith ... and fate.

Both early
and late

Need a break? (Yes)

My chest

feels like it's on fire


(Calling for the death of royalty)

Joyfully... mispronouncing names

(seeking respect)

Recollect ... voices, energy, noises

Centuries,

wasted ...

Memories,

faded

Faces..., the famous

the fakest...,

with fool's gold everywhere.

(Death of a culture)

Someone console her...

she's been raped

(just for having a dream)

At 15...,

I almost killed my father

(Was going to shoot him in his sleep)

How many times must I say...

"Leave me be."

... or they'll be no humanity

(Suffering in sideshows)

Wondering ...

"Who wants to see this?"

Number me ...

666 ...

Now,

time to leave an imprint


"Isn't this what you want?"

We see it every day

"Did the ratings go up?"

Another million in the grave

"Where is this change we we're promised?"

"Where is this greatness?"

I'm here against all of you...

(Only God can save us)

but he ain't in the mood today...

and neither are we


"Will anything ever be pure again?"

How did we get to be here?

On leap year,

my emergence

will call to the virgins...,

(all bleeding)

All seeing...,

eyes will look to me now

The Pharaoh

(The Emperor)

Both loving and sinister

All the bad parts of the Bible...

All the last parts of the cycle

We're caged birds, wondering ...
what it's like to fly

Hunkering... down

Nursing our frowns

(The beginning of the end starts now)


Never seen as helpers...,

just failures

The tales we're ... told

are all fool's gold...,

fooling us into the cold

(Freezing to death)

(Beaten to death)

Teaching us only to fold


Where will be

the next mass casualty?

Catastrophes

(in records)

*Bloodlines*

Get set for,

the going

Now showing

our end

(starring
no one)

barring...,

showmen

"It's too serious for role play."

Roles made ... and gave to us

... the unsaved

Shame on us

for all things

"What if that boy you molested in your dream was really me... in reality... many years ago?"

"How would you know...,
if it wasn't...,

a glitch in the time flow?"

(A skit in a sideshow)

"Let's see how crazy we can make him."

A twist in a dirt road...

a kiss from a dead rose

"We're slaughtered on live T.V."

See me?

I'm live...

then not ... on live T.V.

Not alive...

Here inside...

the grind

of live T.V.

Committed crimes, we are

... on live T.V.

Make believe made to be... real

Names to be filled ... and played

games to our brains

Sync...

but don't blink

(You'll miss the show)

So stop... now go

... off on your own

You're a ship now...,

with no roads home

Always the Christmas peasant

seeking Heaven...

(Trading miracles
for blessing)

No taped audience tonight

We're all alone now...

with the end in sight

Grant us a last request...

... we're all obsessed

with lives... wrecked

So let's check...,

into rehab tonight

and get a rewrite

while the world gets shot up

Pot luck...

dinners

... with cannibals

(Cock sucked)

"Who knows where
the outside is?"

The times we miss...

are made of lines we sniff

(We're not humans)

we're units...

encoded with movement

made to do
whatever it is
we're doing

No proof we're...

intelligent beings at all

Just delicate...

structures

engineering the fall

In the next life
we'll be arrows

flying ... dropping

in scarecrows, rotting

(Just dark days from here)

The coming of age,

the going away

Nothing's the same

anymore ... (all just a war game)

The storm came

... early

Ignored names

... surely

want their faces seen

(Want their words heard)

All backs turned...,

get a beating

followed by the meati-est

parts of their brains, greeted...

with a bullet

"No more quiet time."

(I'm on a roll now)

Reflection ... resurrected


Summer on saddles ...

with rattle ... snakes on yonder

The calmer, ... I get

the farther

we are away from here

"This place is a weapon." (weaponized)

Betting high?

"No way...

this a line that won't change."

(Forever the underdog...,
even though we're favored)


Heed these warnings, please ... I plead,

I beg of thee.

World War Z times 3

(The ending of all things... universal)

Dress rehearsals ... we're all in

Evolved...,

traps ... we fall in

Tripped...,

(mixed with a slip)

Kissed...

only on deathbeds

"I want to be a dictator...,

with an army of gladiators,

each holding a detonator."

(Who's the savior now?)

Who's trending?

(Trading capes for gowns)

Transgending...

"We're really all upside down."

There's no front if in back...

so carry me sideways

There's no want if in fact...

(Scary, this life is)


Flawed failures ... applaud

(You're human now)

Evolved...

silence from the ash

Stashed,

products in a satchel

"Where did the good guys go?"

Capital-lized gains

in blood

(On the doomtrain now)

Love...,

on a new wave now

"How do we make it up there?"

*points to sky*

"How do we make it down here?"

(lost inside)

Only red lights appear

Revered ... faces

tear-ing up...

and facing rain

"Never knew a world this sad."

(Engineered)

Headgear ... needed

My peers ... demons


Dreaming ... of sleeping
stress free

fleeing ...

away from bottom feeders

Problem seekers ...

with numbers

In color ...

the others

from all sides

The fall guy...,

me...

(on hard times)

"How do we get to the top...

when lost
and locked

up ...

to everything we're not?"

Voices ...

say I'm a wizard

In shivers ...

this whole world

A quitter ...

this whole world

It's bitter ...

this whole world

"Who are its defenders?"

"What's that?"

(Something ...

something that's no more)

No door...

leads us to the outside

All floors ... (on fire)

... knees torn ...

(No running today)

The new norm...

... not normal

Through portals

we've fallen

"Immoral?"

(Quite often)

"We are the new today...,

soothed away."

(Now we're just all afraid)


Walls have caved ... in

(Talks delayed)

... but who wants to talk anyway

Stick to the game... plan

(Mind's made)

Click, bang!

Happy Birthday, World!

"Happy earth day."

Career ending ... injury
on the first play
in the first game

of the season

(Buzzer beaten)

Soul searching in a world
that's trick or treating

Freezing water ...

(just to watch it melt)

Somebody else... I am

(Somebody help)

In battles...,
with questionnaires

Testing air

"Okay to breathe?"

(Requesting prayer)

We're in a long line of serpents ...
all standing ...

demanding ...

truth serum ...

(candied)

"Truth hurts 'em."

Landing ... due to emergency

Insurgency ... rising

(Encouraged by timing)

"We all need to wash our hands."

(We're all dirty)

"We all need to cross these sands...,

but aren't worthy ...

enough for the journey


Everyone hurts me...

just to hurt me...

It's funny and serves me ... right

I'm hungry and turning white - ish,
blue-ish, green ...

Slowly ...,

pulling these daggers out

Told we ...,

better not run our mouths

"How dare we complain?"

On bullet trains

we rest now ... afraid to show
our know how

Give us the red letter

Show us the do better

"We can't get an A in this place."

"Destined to remain in this place."

"I don't think we'll ever graduate."

"I don't think we'll ever be the same."

Too much has changed ... and not for the best

Blessings miscounted ...

Betting ... dumbfounded

"Who wants to raise their hand?"

A know it all we need.


Kaleidoscope...,

all colors, painting ... creating
wonder

retaining ... younger

points of view

Joints anew ... (run)

Hoist-ing up guns...

(just to say we're human)

Moving ... at accelerated rates

Our plates,

have enough on them

Highway ... robbery

Ghetto lotteries...

Killing us softly ... all things

costly

"When do we see the son?"


Sleeping through dreams ... we are ...

all beyond means

Who are we outside?

Where are we inside?

No more flags for us

(Ejected)

No more scabs to cut

(Infected)

Somewhere a light

... shines for us

Somewhere a life


Look for me elsewhere

Armchair ... officials

Bare essentials ...,

bearing,
too much weight

Too much take
from all this

So much hate ... in everyone

Buried ones ... we'll soon be

Scary ones... all over.


Gliding with diamonds we are

riding with lions

The finest
of things
we bleed on

Keen on ... something

These claws ... hunting

(Silence near laughter)

If mattered ... you'd see me

heart shattered and screaming out

that I'm a person

(trying to be someone)

Numb from ...

injections

Bummed from ...

beheadings

"I guess it'll all be okay
once in the grave."

Jesus saves, ... right?

(Jesus tames)


Love - 40 ...,

courting ... no one

Poorly ... someone poor

Torn...,

with saviors and swears

(Mourning creators)

Haters ... all over

Favors ... still kosher

"This is the game today."

Paid (off) voices
fill the airwaves

Crazed ... junkies
fill the seats

... next to me... a mirror

that begs to be

a blessed to be item...

Try'n ... to overcome

love,

with the help of a gun

Judgement day closing ... in

soaking in ... reason

going off meaning , thinking
I'm speaking correctly

Correct me, if wrong

I'm testy...,

not sleeping

or sleepy,

needy

or deeply

affected

Just letting

you know in case
there's panic

Waves inside the shade

shaved, safe to say

we're not safe to play

(Owning the grey...,

sorrow ...

ashamed to prey)

"I know I fuck up."

(Adjust the fade)

"Roll credits."

There'll be no sequels here...
or prequels

Sheeple ... we all are

People ... no more


(Selling out to the world)


It's not forced slavery ... it's manipulated.

Why force what can be done voluntarily?

Crumbs are better than nothing.

"Let's give them crumbs!"

(False titles)

"Let's give them some...

false idols ...

only good with balls."

Sports heroes?

Missed free throws ...,
cost us the game again

The chains we're in,

invisible ...

"A grave we're in."


Weeping...,
rotting in a net

"Did Christ stop bleeding yet?"

Not sure...,
those wounds were oh so wide.

Oh so high ... I am...

My, oh my!

"When did tomorrow come?"

"Where was I?"

"Where is tomorrow from?"

"Tears cause I... felt like crying today."

Signing away ... everything

(Sliding away)


Gravitate to me,

to be free ... of frozen grips

Equip me ... please
with guns and many clips

"I think I'll just shoot everyone."

Here we're all at masquerades

It's day time somewhere
but not here

It's playtime! Guns paired ... up
with trigger fingers.

Bitter creatures

in the hearts of most

Hearts of ghost ...,

heartless

invisible

(Parked too close)

The edge...,

we're always on.


Someone message the heavens

"We're dying."

Multiple 187's

residing ... everywhere

All men murderers!

All cripple.

Brittle bones in most

Gross ..., products pending

on war.

"How do we get to the next floor?"

(The stairways on fire)

and next door is Hell.


Aspir-ing to be no one... but me

"Your future king."

Chosen to cream... all your little faces

Traces ... of blood

now everywhere

All scared ...

(I know it)

All bur-
ied up to our eyes
in shit.


Welcome to the freak show

I'm your host

The creepiest of
the creepo's

Zero ...

(You know me)

I'm there when
you're lonely

looking to paint you
black

"We're all crack babies."

(Safely falling)

Lazy to the shaping, gaping
future ... anally assaulted.

"Where's the complaint form?"

(Place needs a new owner)

Showed her ... my dick

Now she's craving for it.

"Yes, I'm a really bad boy."

(All puzzle pieces)

Monster movies

"Jesus, do you see us?"

All are losing ...,

everything

Next we'll say

we all saw it coming

but saw nothing

but a blanket greatly fronting

a world in front of us

A world that isn't just

about the fertile ... women
turned little girls

How many homes in a lifetime?

How many bones in the night time?

We're all at a loss for words

(if not hateful)

We're all just a flock of birds...,

hating as we're instructed.

Here, abducted and trying to reach

ourselves


Fingerprints ... all over

"Lunatics."

Four leaf clovers hang
from my crucifix

New to this
obsession ...,

blessing

"A ruse this is."

Wrecking ...

this room we're in.

"I think I'll let go."

For what?

"Upset with this show."

"Take it off air."

(thuggish, ruggish)

"Too many hateful people on there."

(all just rubbish)

Futuristic...,

when running from the past

(Superstitious)

"Cue the glitches."

The noose is set...,

(actors cast)

It's time to fix
our innocence

or ignore it...

The horrid actions of mankind
are morbid

wishes come to life

"What have we become?"

It's all madness

stabbing our own children

Spilling their blood all over

Our shoulders ...,
sore from all the torture

"Nun's bleeding...,

between the
legs..., and sees me

peeking
at her reset

The sheet's wet ...

change it!

(The freak's dead)

All I wanna do
is travel ...

(see the aurora)

Fuck bitches at Sodom

and Gomorrah

Pandora's ... box

this world is

"Does anyone have a cheat code?"

The beasts know we're here

for their amusement

(Entertaining)

"A kiss for every fuse lit."

(Finger banging)

Deadly..,

getting

far too heavy

"Begging...

to adjust the settings."

(Option mode - insane)

"Put it on easy."

Need me ... do you?

"I see ... through you."

"Here's your admittance to innocence

in case you missed it."

(Here's your penitence)

Forgetting I'm to grieve all ... victims ... born to parish

Tariffs...,

even on the soul

The sold ... out

trolled ... false polled

(Shovels of modern age)

"Puddles are here to stay."

No comfort in headlocks

Sweatshops ... we're all in

(thinking we're living)

Crumbs we're getting ...
saying it's a feast

Into bits ... we venture

Simp-ler times extinct

In this crime, asleep ...

(but just as guilty)

Just as filthy
as all past "primitive" cultures

"Who's gonna hose us down,

show us how... to be someone?"

"We're gonna close up now."

Silencing the lambs...

tightening the clamps

Advanced ... (only to the ants)

No more fortunes for us...,

just graves ... on Mars.

No more organs in us...,

just change ... we are

(under the same dollar)

"Worth just
a cent more
than worthless."

Upside down, ... shirtless ... giving

reach arounds to all

our pedo masters


It's what it is
and no more
than that

"The happily ever after?"

(Not us)

"The meaning of this chapter?"

(We're fucked)

"Hope you know how to swim..., kill."

"Hope you know how to skim... across slaughter."

Most ... bother me

No ... honor left in society

Dear Father ... God,

we're conquered.

(Help us in double time)

The twisted I ... screaming

The lifted lie...

Feeding...

between the thighs

while bleeding

(All is perfect now)

Six, six, me ... plus 6

Imprints ...

of wings ... incensed ... with
many things

(all which are divisive)

Delighted,

we still have dreams

Excited,

we still love things

(Though most are evil)

In 50 years
our sins
won't be sins
anymore.

The law won't allow it.

"I need an allowance."

(Got priests to pay)

... Busting up mountains ...

(the easy way.)

"Regaining ...,
hope to believe in."


Much needed

this rest... Reques - ting

heads... to put bullets in

Morticians ... rejoice!

"You're never
going out
of business."

All defensive ... players

line up

(You're on offense now)

The lost and found..., lost
... when found

Shot down...,

we'll all be

crossed out


None more beaten than those

that won't grow ... up

and don't know ... why

Resign ...

we have to

In line ...

for crap shoots

(hoping they're not a gamble)

In scandals ... all

Dismantled ... laws

... sinister

Fatal flaws...

finishers

Pass me the ball

and I'll stab it

Dagnabbit...,

the world's coming down.

"My only wish is that yours come true."

Hung through...

all of this together

We never see
the blessings
in front of us

until we look back

(Feet trapped)

The wrong path ...

we seem to always take

Always late

we are

"Never safe."

Not in a rush,
just ready to go

Ready to leave here

Ready to grow

Messy,

the night time

Testy,

our bones

Broken

we all are

Requesting a home

Stoned on a dead end... road ... deadened

... messing up
myself on purpose

Burdens...,

adding up

Burning...,

every fuck - ing thing

I get my hands on.

Planned on ... coming

but felt like running

Danced with ... bloody
money on a Sunday

(Wicked air)

Breath of the dragon

(Fisting bare)

"Backing action."

This whole world is smoking ...
but not inhaling

This whole world is broken ...

(all have gone crazy)

Worth saving?

"Prove it."

Our useful - ness
is at an end


What if we're the cumshot ... swimming

Survival of the fittest ... getting

more than we bargained for

(The earth is a womb)

Heart hardened ... screws loose

(Soft targets,

we all are)

"The end's started."

No great generations here...

just raped ones

Contagious... is hatred

The sane ones...,

brainwashed

Ungracious ... for their sanity

First in line
last in the building
Fielding these errors
Terror strikes make a killing
Everyone's kneeling
Meds need filling
Peeling off grins, skins
hanging from the ceiling
Most now bleeding
Here daydreaming
Hoping crumbs flee, leak
free for a feeding
Eating as leaches
sucking out reason
We are the first cursed
worst of the beings
Less hearts beating
More mouths screaming
Covered in semen, demons
preaching to the heathens
Freeing up legions
Eden's still grieving
Treasonous teachings, keeping
us in pieces.


Don't forgot your coat

It's cold outside

Never mind the sunshine

98?

Hate ... (keeps it cold outside)

Welcome to the picnic

The twisted wish this
wasn't a picnic

Sadistic... these matters

Complicit... our masters

(We of the burning summer)

Younger ... we can't be

Slumber ... we'll all see

The last sleep

coming ...

Best not blink


Licking in 6's...

(clitoris)

Kicking in fences

The shore just ...

swallowed the ocean down

Rainbows ... wrapped around
flamethrowers

Came sober ... went insane

Game over

"Everyone feels pain

in this grain ... of salt ... named

Earth."


I walk across the air sometimes ... all of you below me ...
unknowing ... that I'm above you ... showing ...
my dick to the world.

(Here comes the rain)

What have we gained... aside for more people to blame ... for
everything

Don't say I'm beautiful, that's sexist

*Bloodlines*

The guest list ... includes the headless

Infected ... are messes ... connected to guesses

"Everywhere the front line now."


The exits ... are all packed

The edits ... are in fact..., credits...
wiretapped

Wires back, peeled

Wires snapped

We've got a long way to go till tomorrow

A long road

(Anything can happen)

A dark zone

Watch who you call a friend

"You never know."

"They may just be a demon."

On a hill...

the fog covers me

(I'm underneath it)

It's water but I can breathe it

"We're the only creatures here."

(No roommates)

"We're the only feature here."


Predicting this downfall was easy ...

I've seen it a thousand times

Altered states of mind in circles

(wishing for candied rain)

Ramming planes ... into stadiums packed

(Damning change)


Here we are now as candles, melting

wax ... upon the face.

"No real way out of this."

This town it is... a glue trap we're born on.

Storms come ... daily

Torn up ... babies

laying in garbage cans.

"Who's in charge here?"

"How do we reach them?"

(Everywhere a foreign land)

Not at home here...,

or a welcomed guest

We seldom get ... rain

(unless we beg for it)

The legs for this race ...,

we don't have

"How will we reach the finish?"

Repentance...,

we surely need.


Surely we will make it

(Won't we?)

I can't be

the only one

fighting for the lonely

We matter ... don't we?

(Hope we ... do)

Know the phony

must get going

(No room for traitors)

King slayers...,

heroes

(Game savers)

This quest?

"Holy."

Boldly ... going

where no man has before

(Scabs galore)

"Can't help it."

(What's the score?)

"Still losing?"

(Where's the door?)

"It's time to leave

and time to be ... someone

other than me

(Time to feed)

... honorary cannibals

"All must bleed."

"What will be your reason for hating me today?"

Hating what you made.

I wish it all away..., again.

Wish I wasn't afraid..., to live.

Wish I knew how to play...,

had friends.

Wish I knew what to say...

when praying ...

All that I know .... is "sorry."

Card me...

I'm underage.

Underpaid...

Under everything...

Impossible to fly when chained up

(Un-dottable the i's)


Everyone hopes for something

(Even tyrants)

Heightened...,

to new heights

Still killing Christ ... this world

still under ice

"I wonder why
that I don't
wonder why."

Guess that I ... will just be a hero ... fallen

Stalling ... anything holy


Hold me..., I'm hurting

Hurt... cause they burned me.

How many times must I welcome you to today?

(Face mask needed)

All here freezing ... to death
in this wicked place

This game of chase

... chaotic ...

This game of fakes

All on the inside now

... no comments ...

We're as the houseflies now


Roll out the red carpet ...

(The end's started)

No pardons here...

just targets

*Bloodlines*

Just darkness

fills the daytime

Playtime's over

Here, the half Joker draws

visions in the bloodlines

Sometimes the fall ...

is easy to point out.

Noise down...,

we need sleep

It's too loud and bad dreams ...

are all we seem to have

Name tags

filling up the dumpsters

In drag...,

painting with the numbers


"When will we be the special ones?"

This schedule runs ... too deep

Too beat to be me...

(Follies)

News fixed for T.V.

(Zombies)

"We'd all be evil ... if allowed to."

(Time to raise our statue)

The map to ... the exit's

an artist's rendition

We'll have to go back to

the first beginning


Where to put our feet?

Where to take our steps?

(There'll be nothing to lose
once nothing is left)

Where to dig our graves?

Where to put our guns?

(There'll be no one to save
once everyone's hung)


(Face me)

Face to face we ...,

see the ...delay we...

put on things

(Hook to things)

Changing ... hate we

say we think we ...

got it under control

(Underneath holes)

The maybe's paint the

chains we ...

keep on our souls

(All hearts cold)


"Better get those prescriptions filled ...

we have a long road ahead."

(Zones)

A long line of red...,

(bloody) Bones

guide the missiles

Rise of temples long lost ... ancient...,

all stops..., tainted

What channel are we on?

What station?

Who's planet are we on?

(Much hatred)

"We have many things to take care of."

Be aware of
everything...,
under the sun ...,

when the heart breaks

The sharks wake ...,

hungry

The cards lay ...,

funny

"I think they've been tampered with."

"Who here's a hustler?"

"Who here's disabled?"

In cradles ...,

the future

despite all

the rumors

"We still have a claim here."

The change here?

"Customary."

(Much hate here)

The chains here?

"Temporary."

(No slaves here)


I don't wanna walk on water ...,

just alters of pedophiles

calling themselves "father."

How do we get to the 7...,

when mess'n around too much we do ...

with Armageddon?

I think we need to relax...,

remove the knives from our back

and count backwards till we reach...

the front.

Leave the stunts ... to them

(Bleed the cunt)

"We're all shadows now...,

with scissors."

"We're all cattle now."


"Still waiting on the good guys?"

End time ... goodbyes

to all...

(Outside the reply)

Outside the sunshine...,

dissolved ...

alongside the downsize

"Kill the pope."

It'll help the show's ratings

"Cut his throat."

So what if I'm a monster!

(A mon-star)

"Get ready for the slaughter... or don't

bother ... to do anything ...

but get conquered"

(It may be your role to play)

Holes to bang ... many

(souls to save)


Line's hooked to something

"I think we need a guidebook."

(Flight's booked)

"Let's get out of here."

"Let's go everywhere."

"I can't be here no more."

Uniform ... on.

Time to get gone...,

I'm going ...

Time? (A test for all)


Recalled ... this planet

We've manned it

and totally fucked it up.

Why are we like this?

Are we in the matrix...,

reliving our coming end?

The currents shift ...,

slither

(This record skips ...
change it)

A sinking ship ...,

we're on.


50% right ...

50% wrong ...

Stay calm

If lost,

I'll find you

(Doppelgängers)

"Familiar strangers."

Leader of this new night

The moonlight

chose me...

to keep skies holy

(Preacher of this new fight)

"I think there's a pathway somewhere
that leads to a door."

That bleeds with the Lord ... stitched up.

Sees the before and after

Fear factors ... everywhere

Boos loud as usual

(Mute the sound)

"Fuck the crowd!"

In fear you're beautiful

All is now ...,

upside down

"I have no place among you."

I've clung to ... things that I didn't want to

... just to have a feeling

(Be alive)

Coming now the villains ...

(dead inside)

All in stride my people

"All in time."


"Who paid for this script?"

This bit..., worn out

This skit..., over

(Time to get off this ship)

This trip... wasted.

"When will we ever learn, and

ever turn back to loved ones?

"Where is the red fern ... growing?"

(My dogs are dead)

The gods defect ...

(Why not?)

All is wrecked..., fucked

All in debt


Who planted the first seed?

The first me..., thirsty ...

for first things

(First)

Worse things flirt ...

with cursed things

Hurt things learn

from burnt things

(Cells) ... offspring

(Bells) ... won't ring

"No saving here."

(Just hating)

Never know the backstabbers until after...,
they pull out the dagger.

What is the factor here?

"What is the matter?"

(I'm not looking for your message)

Confession..., to men

not headed anywhere

Many hairs grey now

Empty chairs ...,

at funerals


"When did we become so selfish... or are we really just
shellfish ... alone at the bottom... eating ourselves?"


I dreamt of demons again the other night...here to kill off
mankind and mankind helping them to do so.

I saw all of my past friends in this dream, from all ages.

(It was nice to see their faces)

Too bad those faces were the last thing I saw
as they betrayed me and helped the demons kill me off.

(Same as reality)

Here scalping things for comfort.

(These battle scenes ...

you're all in)


Curiosity didn't kill the cat...

this track did

Reaction ... to this trip

was classic... storytelling in the making

I'm taking ...

a day off from everything

Candy canes ...,

no different than menstrual stains

(wrapped in plastic)

All in caskets ... eventually

unless blasted

... away

Perversion ...

in first person (P.O.V)

We don't see ... the outside things

turnin'

until urgent. Squirtin'

cumshots everywhere

Servin' ... seeds to vampires

An outsider? (Always)

A pit viper

"I guess I'll just take my leave."

*Bloodlines*

The bottom sees ...

the top

more than we do

We seem to ...,

not see much of anything

(but pain)

Blood drained ...

We are... gang banged

(Hating every facial)

(Sore from all the anal)

Tamed and unable to detect

betrayal

Labeled ... we all are

Angels ... we need

How many screams till mercy?

Blood spurting ... hurry!

(We're hurting)

Unheard we must be

cursed. Combusting...,

spontaneous

All craziness

this way...

"All babies blessed."


I don't care if you hate me...

you'll be told to anyway

The gold you seek is fake.

"Fool. It's me that's the snake

hunting... That one something...

no one sees

coming."

Steady pumping...

venom in the bloodstream

"Sin to keep a cut clean...,

if they make it."

(Soon to be a fucked thing)

Robots,

waiting to kill us...

(Part of the narrative)

Comparative?

(Suicide)

Mood's described ... as

doomed inside

Screwed are we?

(Maybe)

Proof that we're

changing ...

into killers

(Changed)

Banging ... holes

(dismembered)

Brains

"Yes, we're the burden

worsen-ing the current

structure of things."

Fucked her and came ...

right in her little ass

(Hashtag needed)

Silently screaming...,

inside

Privately...,

beaten


It's nothing that's anything more than it is.

The sores on our wrists ...,

inherited.

(Born to split lips...,

below belts)

"Born to sink ships."

I don't mind being the dragon...,

being the kraken ...

(Summon me)

Bringing some action

(to comedy)

"Adding some caption."

This is where the next level starts

Our best vessel...,

needed

Distress signals

tweeted ... (hoping)

to reach God.


I'm not a robot,

I'm a cumshot

(solving captcha)

About to fax a ...

meaning to the end

Seeming just to blend

right in

Keeping track of grins...,

twisted

Len's ...,

lifted

"I see you."

Form...,

weaving

Here,

being...

whatever seen mess
I walk as


Everyday judgement...,

everyday people

Everyday, all day
threading the needle

"How will we get our clothes back?"

The road's packed ... and bad.

Where's home at?

(Frustration)

No making
it out
of this thing
alive

Invasions ...,

... everywhere

Here stationed ......, alone, marooned

Out of time and room......

(Soon starving)

Moon's hardening
up
for one more go...

One more show..., enjoy it

"Time to close."


Illusions and detours...

(all this world is)

Along with clenched fists,

threats

and heads filled
with nonsense

"Who's in charge of this experiment?"

Steering this ride...,

not us

Pyramids guide

what tucks ...

us in
when mothers fail

Under Hell

we could be

Shotgun shells...,

we are

Lost ones sail

universal...

undiscovered...,

'round the clutter

in perfect color.

In perfect pitch

we scream

for supper ...

Hoping some other's

feeding the buzzards

"Here goes a sex tape."

Our best days ...

(gone)

with less days

(ahead)

Invested ...

only in regret

Phony as it gets

(this system) Just

bones we

have to show


Care if your heart stops?

"I don't."

Paired with this time slot,

unknown ...

programming

Grandstanding

we are

Disbanding ...

purpose

"We won't know if there'll be a tomorrow...
until it comes."

Till then we'll plunge

continuous...

Till then we'll hunt


The moon grieves every sunset...

cause every day gets ... harder

and every truth gets farther ...

away from being the truth


We're all tired
and hungry.

"Didn't we used to be something?"

We're all liars
and junkies...,

evolving back to monkeys.


Growing up, we're not really given different points of view,
alternative ways of thinking or any other ways to see things.

We're taught to think one way and one way only.

We are given grades based on this way of thinking.
Accept what we tell you and pass. Question what
we tell you and fail.

Thing is, you're taught only the answers they give
and through this, taught not to ask questions.

Why is this?

Shouldn't we be asking questions?

We're lied to all the time by our news media, politicians,
teachers, celebrities, priest..., even our own loved ones. Then
told we're stupid or crazy for questioning it.

How deep does the lie go?

What world have they created around us?

We have translations based on translations of translations
based on more translations that we are then told to accept
as documented facts.

Our history is made up by our conquerors.

And theirs?

By the conquerors before them.

For all we know we're going nowhere in a circle or everywhere on a line.

Crazy how we're the ones that will witness the end.


Here we are now

back to this loss...,

of sanity

Humanity ...

described best with

profanity

"Fuck everyone."

No dance that we

will ever be

invited to

Excited to...

kill everything

"Good riddance."

*Bloodlines*

Most shit list

include forgiveness

Groomed to end this

whole...

doomed existence


The cannibals started chasing me. I remember running
into some building trying to lose them but ended up just
running into a trap.

One leaped down from the ceiling in front of me and 3 from
behind grabbed me. I closed my eyes and felt their teeth
taking chunks out of me. I felt the flesh being torn away
from my shoulders and heard their teeth chewing it up.

Fading to black, I slowly woke up..., then quickly ...
still feeling them around me.


Some of the worst people in the world are in this room...,

and they're all me

I'm fall-ing

back to fall guys

No sight,

set on me

(Trash in all eyes)

Lift up the bottom ...

it's on us

We're pawns just...,

pretending to be kings

Pretending to have queens

(instead of whores)

Pretending everything

is ok

(Defending every scream)

How do we know where the good ones are?

Withstood so far...,

temptations

of permanent

vacations

Who do the good ones star?

(I don't know their names or faces)

In mazes,

us all

(Cum traces)


This stage is

getting smaller...

crowded

It's time to
announce that ...,

"I have a hand-
grenade."

(Heads to bang)

"We'll have an escapade."

(Crusade)

"Give me some fucking credit!"

I'm still here..., somehow

And still cheer...

for all of the bad guys

All are in scabs (Highs...

and lows

keep us level)

"I guess."

I prefer to hurt less

but whatever

Aggressors ...

come in all shapes and sizes

Still surprised I've

yet to run amok

Tails are tucked ...

(from spankings)

Tails are fucked.


"Free me!" she said

Judge Dredd like (except not)

Eyes red,

I'm dead

(Spies tread)

"We are the next and going."

Necks are showing ...

(teeth marks)

Less are growing.

"We need to find our whereabouts."

The air's about ... out

I think we might drown

Trying to find a genie

(Three wishes)

Can't see me

Suspicious... minds,

defenseless

Offended ...

by everything


Here... nowhere

(Going through the motions)

Explosive ...

all things

Omens ...

I see

Slightly

coming...

Timing's

money

"Here we fall again."

(Are again)

Alienated ...

At our breaking point

Elevated ...,

just to be dropped down.


An unexamined life is a wasted one

In case we're done here...,

this stay was one

we'll never forget

Indoctrinated for how long

have we been?

Painstaking

arguments...,

(with idiots)

"Names taken."


We're not living

We're existing

(There's a difference)

Within me...,

admittance ...

to many promised lands

"I'm cooling."

Many empty stands

"We're dueling."

(Things just not the same)


What if we went back in time only to find cultures so
advanced ... they make us the primitive one?

Manufactured visions of the future...,

implanted

(help water down the past)

There will be no antiques for us to purchase
when we're old ...

cause nothing these days last.

# **Psalms**

I saw my mom dreaming of me as a baby.

She sounded so happy yet so sad.

I went back to my room and pretended to be a baby.

"I'm nothing but a fuck up."

The snakes bit me in my hands last night.

(They bit me hard all in my fingers.)

My dad showed me this timeline he made on a poster board.

It was my birth to my death.

He said that he envisioned it.

My mom sees me as a baby…,

my dad sees me dead…

but the funniest thing about it all is…

none of them see me now.

I don't know
how much more
I can take
or keep inside

All I feel,
all I am
is a tear
unmeant to dry

I don't know
what it's like
to be loved
by anyone

People are
nothing more
than a waste
of blood and cum


I actually saw the sun today

(First time in awhile)

Millions of miles away,
await...

the shape of another ache

Time to start walkin'

to a new place

where days don't pass
if happy

Trapping...,

each little smile
I can

(Cuts to the bone)

Thoughts of being sad...,
periods...,
tongues and bloody rags

(mud between toes)

My own...,

place to feel
at home

"Nowhere."

Just a snake in the water.

My nose…,

will it ever stop bleeding?


Severed from the seasons

Hopelessly decreasing

Quickly I'm the weakest

in the world

In last though I'm leading

Everyone is bleeding

Opening the deep end

of the world

Naked and uncovered

Tucked away from summer

Screaming with the thunder

at the world

Silence without color

Prayers heard, I wonder?

The days soon to slumber

Fuck the world


Just like crickets.

We are

no different

(Just crushed in harder ways)

Father stayed    drunk.

Father fades...,

to black

"Paint the picture."

"Taint the scripture."

Not new to things getting ruined.

Use to it ...

by now

(Groomed for it)


Guts on the road

"I think I just saw God explode."

( Pissed at humanity )

I'm cold
on the inside

and out

( Form of an S )

I'm out of things to guess

"My head hurts,
soul hurts."

Feel I have
no worth,
to anyone

"Leave me."

(On the run)

"Needing...,

everyone."


She will never
come to me

I will never
run to her

On the other side
of all that's me...,

do days move differently?

She will never
fall for me

Maybe I'm too
wrong for her

On the other side
of all we see…,

does love come easily?

She will never
reach for me

Maybe I'm too
far from her

On the other side
of what can't be…,

do tears mean anything?

She will never
feel for me

I guess I'm just
shit to her

On the other side
of life she'd be…,

still way too good for me


27 footprints in the sky

27 lingering goodbyes..., departing

"Is it possible to run away
in two different directions?"

(Going nowhere)

Imaginary friend so eager to leave
I don't blame you, I know it's me
you hate

27 frozen emotions

27 prayers unfocused..., none of them matter

"Inside I'll never stop crying."

"It seems my tears erect this earth"

Bent shade reflects fear

How many more faces do I have to see
of people smiling happily
except me?

27 screams a day..., all at myself

27 words in grey...

Am I part of this creation,
cursed wherever I'm located

All the one's I thought were special
were a tool used by the devil

I don't know what keeps me going

(Must be something that's not showing)

In my head a million voices

Every tear that falls is poisoned

Am I just a false illusion
trapped within a lost conclusion?

In and out of sane decisions
stuck inside a self-made prison

God on me, no one is leaning

Life I feel has lost its meaning

Seems I'm here just to be hated

King of all that is degraded

16 wishes of
cross shaped tears

Ruling forever
in the movement of a sigh

Filling the budding air,

(anonymous)

A name in no one's prayers


Today I'll turn
into the rain
and wash you all
the fuck away

Slamming doors and beating drums

Soon to kill myself for fun

Today I'll dive
up out the sky
Just so you
can see me die

This you've prayed
a million times

"Guess that makes it
homicide."

"No one knows what makes me feel okay."

Everything is dangerous

Wish I had a million bucks

"Sometimes I'd just like to fade away."

Reaching for a booby trap

Needing just a little nap

"I wish I could ease across the day."

All your dreams too good for me

I am just a casualty

"Please just find a place for me to lay."

Somewhere by a holy man

(Innocence upon the sand)

"I doubt X will ever mark the spot."

Everything I wish to have

lost inside a garbage bag

"Here we are another heartbeat lost."

All we love is history

wrapped inside a rotting tree

"What's it like to have a happy thought?"

I doubt I will ever know

where the hell the flowers grow

"Everything I heard was true is false."

Guess that makes me stupid now

On my way to going down.

All I see are raindrops...,

falling on clowns

Discovering...,

new ways to drown

everything important

In madness,

I was born to be

(Black lights in my soul)

Glowing... twisted

heart of a troll

Unable to bring forth meaning

I'm deeming...,

this place
a hazardous
waste

Lights off
.........
Dead...,

wrapped in a leaf

A king to be?

"Never"

Just bones
in broken feet

Cold...,

on the other side of sun

Soon to run...,

backwards
in the night sky

Ghost towns of salt ...

(All gods disabled)

A throbbing cock
robbing
love from
a cradle

Deciding to bleed
my wishes…,

next to holy screams

(World full of lice)

Nothing's nice
if human

I'm pukin'

love I've never shared

"Help me!"

I'm yelling

at the top of my lungs…

but no one comes

(As usual)

I've tricked myself again…


I'm just a cartoon in her world…

My love's not real,
too many cold chills

I'm no good for this girl…

The uncrowned queen
in need of a king

Fishin' for sunken pearls...

Making a wish
in lieu of a glitch

Causing the mind to swirl...

Sleepin' on weeds
defended by screams

Breaking my body down...

Twistin' my head
with cries of the dead

Silent within a sound...

Lost in the words
of "this life for hers"

Missin' her face year 'round...

Filling my heart
with poisonous darts

Hiding behind a frown...

Scared to dream of
finding true love

Nothing can help me now

Who sits home...,
left behind?

Hiding in the cracks
of a smile that lies

Each day's the same when
you're barely alive

Who now cries to pass time?

Stranded on a ship that's destined to sink...

Hating everything that's allowed to think...

No one to talk to but my shrink...

Even my laughter's filled with kinks

Who here hates the way they look?

Feelin' like a worm
upon a hook

Lost in the pages of
children's books

Who here feels that God's a crook?

Prayin' for a peace that'll never come...

Walking to the beat of a different drum…

Hating myself for fucking fun…

(Wondering why do these days come)

Who here feels they don't belong?

Strugglin' for ways
to just keep calm

Feeling more and more
part of this song?

Who can't tell what's right from wrong?

Every time I wake I want to cry…

Whenever I dream, I always die…

Constantly I'm asking

"Dear God why…

can't these days
just ease on by?"

Who's real close to giving in?

Unable to taste
the sweetest sin

Spilling their guts
out through a pen

Who can't wait till these days end?


The hills of heaven have a name...

"Three wishes"

Need stitches...,

to reconnect my brain

Broke dishes...,

clogging up the soul

I'm told,
the future's been put
on hold

(My goodness)

"Hey God,
how are you?"

Not speaking?

I think your tears
are leaking
feeding
the fires
of hell

No feelings...,

only a sour smell

(Corroded)

"Why are these days so hard?"

Hands held out
reaching for limbo

Seen as a ghost
trapped in a window

Concrete soul in hand

I stand...,
shattered...

"The brokest man."

No one is here
dancin' with me

Answers I find
only in screams

Yellin' so loud...

"King of boo-hoo's"

Only born to
be nothing and lose

No one is here
praying for me

Guess I'm not meant
to have anything

here in my life...

Knife in my chest

Seems each day I
care even less

No one is here
calling for me

Nowhere is where
I think I may be

Taking up space

(Piles of bones)

Purpose on earth?

"Being alone."

No one is here
searching for me

Maybe I'm too
dirty to see

Lower than shit
covered with flies

Worthless I am
in everyone's eyes


Burdens on my shoulders

like boulders

falling into a crowd

Ka-pow!!

"I'm nothing now"

(Never was)

Just a person
to cuss
at

"Fuck you!"

Do I deserve
such kindness?

My life is
nothing you'd like
to know

(Wars in an ink pen)

My soul, I think
is covered by a snake's skin

Unable to give off rays

Away…,

goes another day

Living through all
that's dead...

(Piss on my hands)

There's a hook through my tongue
in the shape of a man

ripped in half

"I think I'm gonna cry."

Why?

"I cannot say"


Abandon me
when freedom rings
so I can soar
with my own wings

Through violet skies
and orange clouds

As pure as prayer
from virgin mouths

I'm just a boy
from no one's earth

Inside a way
that no one's learned

Beneath the stars
on cloudy nights
just hoping for
a glimpse of light

I see myself
in drops of rain
unknown to all
who bear a name
inside the heart
of Christian grace
pretending its
a special place

Unwanted, "Yes"
I'm not allowed
within the arms
of happy crowds
so I must go
where I can be
what no one's eyes
will ever see


Born to not be right?

It seems so

The wind blows...,

only when light
goes night

The main show
features the
out of sight

I don't know...,

what makes thoughts
so bright

Here to not be sane?

Most likely

Fighting...,

stains that fill
my brain

Enlightened?

Life a twisted
game

I'm finding...,

pleasure within
my pain

Seen as just a joke?

Unhappy

Soul just feels
piss soaked

I'm jabbing...,

nails into my throat

Relaxing...,

hoping that you
all choke

Soul to rot in hell?

I hope not

Laced with poisoned
snails

I forgot...,

how to make
things well

A whole lot...,

I just seem
to fail


Somewhere in
the distant past

I think I
was broken glass

in the feet
of Christian kings

cursing me
from holy things

I don't have
a hand to lend

or the strength
to be a friend

I don't know
what love can do

All I know
is I'm not you

Picture me
inside your mind

head chopped off
without a spine

nailed on to
a rotting tree

finding God
lost at sea

I can't tell
the real from fake

I feel like
a soulless snake

Dreaming still
to one day be

something that
you people need


God of unseen faces...,

my calling,

a wasted piece of time

In the sky?

Fragments of my mind

(Eaten by the birds)

If needed,
I will be here
with guns drawn,
facing the day
as my conscience lays
next to the bible

(Gifts upon arrival)

Nails through the feet

My face…,
covered by a sheet

dirty…,
with piss stains on it

Undaunted

The screams…,

closing in on me

(Six feet in the sand)

Two moons on the rise

"Where is the seventh day?"

(Good question)

A place where
the demons play?

"Earth."

(Sporting an evil grin)


I envy those in love

I envy those that laugh

I envy those that know themselves
and don't live in the past

I envy those that hope

I envy those that dream

I envy those with Christian hearts
who pray for better things

I envy words of grace

I envy tears of joy

I envy all the special things
that make you say "oh boy"

I envy new todays

I envy happy thoughts

I envy all the fields of gold
that put the soul in knots


The truest of all stories
are told in children's books...,

Innocent and unknowing

(Creative retribution)

Your true colors are showing...,
with no color at all

Innocence stands
with a noose around its neck
waiting for a name to grab

Wishing God was here

(Postcards to heaven)

I once dreamt that Adolf Hitler
crucified me to a concrete wall.

Thousands witnessed and cheered
and didn't shed one tear
as the life gave up in me.

(Society represented)

"Who exists to who?"

(Decapitating kisses)

How do you stand tall
when you can't stand at all?

Names in the fire
along with my youth...,

(I guess it's time to melt)

Faith is made
of cough drops...,

hearts are made
of ash...,

somewhere there's
a vomit bag
stinking up
the trash

Looking just like me...,

attracting only flies


There's no drug in the world
I'm good enough
to be on...,

or voice in the world
I'm good enough
to hear.

No death in the world
I'm good enough
to cry for...,

or thought in the world
I'm good enough
to clear

There's no dream in the world
I'm good enough
to walk through...,

or chance in the world
I'm good enough
to take.

Nothing in the world
I'm good enough
to try for…,

or choice in the world
I'm good enough
to make

There's no god in the world
I'm good enough
to call to…,

or hope in the world
I'm good enough
to have.

No one in the world
I'm good enough
to think of…,

or hand in the world
I'm good enough
to grab

There's no face in the world
I'm good enough
to look at…,

or word in the world
I'm good enough
to say.

No change in the world
I'm good enough
to pray for…,

or place in the world
I'm good enough
to stay


Who's the man behind the curtain?

Cumstained on a bed of nails?

Dripping down a plastic chain?

Hoping for a thought to sale?

Who's the man entwined in urine?

Pouring salt into his wounds?

Lusting for a way to breathe?

Winning only if he'll lose?

Who's the man tied down to freedom?

Greased up with a demon cock?

Playing in a bed of ants?

Binded to a golden lock?

Who's the man inside the mirror?

Cutting up the things he sees?

Going nowhere but straight down?

Happy only when he bleeds?


Selfish ways
and never dids

Sometimes it seems
that's all there is

Blackened eyes
and bloody lips

Sometimes it seems
that's all there is

Hurtful thoughts
and bleeding wrists

Sometimes it seems
that's all there is

Broken hearts
and shitty friends

Sometimes it seems
that's all there is

Evil deeds
and holy shits

Sometimes it seems
that's all there is

Rainy days
and dying kids

Sometimes it seems
that's all there is


Stars on a wall
too bright to fall

Secrets above us all

The meaning of life?

Shh...,

don't tell anyone

Right on the tip
of my tongue…,

the barrel of a gun

(sodomized by laughter)


I slit my wrists'
for a penny
to give to the needy,
then walked all night
on the highway
hoping to get hit

"I will never love you!"

She said so clearly

"Turning my world
to shit."

(A step away from hell)

Voices from a bell…,

demonic…

Taking my mind away

through answers,
never meant to be

Wrapped around my mouth,
an eye that cannot see

anything

Angels I've wished for
to save me so long
with a love from a place
where nothing is wrong

In tune with my heart

Full moons in my bed

The angels won't come.

The angels are dead

"What am I left to live for?"


Bent Christian,
full of vision

Lead me to
a good intention

One worth having

(feelings stacking)

In my soul,
a smile cracking

Winged circle,
blue and purple

Take me to
a different world

Free of power

All that's sour

Broken bones
and worthless hours

Burnt laughter,
here and after

Watch the way
a feeling shatters

into pieces

New diseases

In my head
a crying Jesus

Freed crazies
holding babies
over holes
that lead to Hades

Bodies droppin'

Future's rotten

All we have is
what's forgotten


Blood drips
when a wish
is made upon a star

Who are we?

Who cares

(Food for hungry bears)

Turning into shit...

Souls on a giant scab,

lost in the same place as love

( Nowhere )

New voices,
mystery,

all doors closed

Less reasons to live
all over again

"This day…has been a long one."

Laid out on a picnic table…

My hatred

Keeping your bellies full

(Awaiting the stings of a bee)

The wounds of Christ…,

still bleeding

Tears we've yet to cry

As rivers dry

New days…,

next to never come


Facts, they hurt me

I'm nothing.

( I know )

Curse the ground that I walk on

( The ways that I go )

Love, it breaks me

I'm stupid.

( I know )

Curse the days that accept me

( The things that I know )

Eyes, they hate me

I'm ugly.

( I know )

Curse the hands that I reach to

( The tears that I show )

Life, it kills me

I'm worthless.

( I know )

Curse the things that I live for

( The seeds that I sow )

Pain, it seeks me

"Deserve it."

I know

Curse the ones that I bleed for
and those that I don't

Death, it wants me

( You're happy )

I know

Curse all that's above me...,

and all that's below

Broken glass
and plastic frames
are all that keep
the passing pain
away from eyes
that hurt the most
from a heart
completely broke

Rotten wood
and rusty nails
are all that hold
the inner self
together at
its strongest parts...

Right around
the dying heart...

( Sour in the middle )

A man I hope to
someday be,
but first I need
a soul

Fool's gold…,

wrapped around the world

( Smells of a rotting cow )

My mouth…,

spits on all who smile

Laughing with God…,

talking of execution

Seclusion…,

a word I know so well

Here in a holy hell

My mind…,

torn between realms

Love?

( Less than an ounce )

Life?

( No longer counts )

"What's the point of trying anymore?"

A whore

I am for sin


Welcome to
the slaughterhouse

Broken hearts
are selling out

Cheaper than
a bloody mouth

Who's to stop
the crying now?

Everyone
is fast asleep

Drained of all
they claim to be

In a trance
beneath the sea

Nailed to rocks
inside of me

Welcome to
the things at hand

Everyone's
too weak to stand

Dearest God
I must demand
some part in
your holy plan

Seems I'm lost
in who I'm not

Thinking that
I'm just a dot

To the sky
I cry a lot

Asking if
I'm all I've got

Welcome to
the failing mind

*Bloodlines*

In a war
with human kind

On the edge
a million times

Hanging from
a dying vine

All my words
come from below

Where the light
will never go

Stuck inside
a dying crow

Hoping for?

"I don't know"


A wall of mirrors...,

broken

( Helping the truth be seen )

Vendettas...,

surrounded by screams

Soon to find Jesus?

"I guess."

"Am I allowed to?"


If the day ever comes
when I cry for another...

the ground
will be still
no more

As the tears of the devil
hunt for a lover...

why is my heart so sore?

If my arms ever brace
the warmth of another...

the sun
will come up
no more

For the touch of the devil
burns like the summer...

*Bloodlines*

What do the birds sing for?


My tears would reign forever
if they could drown this earth

A seven day moon…

the unknown right

( Arms now crossed )

In heaven they gripe…,

"What's this world coming to?"

( Chambers of dreams )

sleep occurs

Impossible things...,

we hope for


Trust me...

even if you think

I'm cra-zy

Give into instinct

I'm lone-ly

hiding from heartbreak

and don't need

another soul shake

It's hopeless

gunning for something

unfoc-used

Tired of running

A sure miss...

Chances I'm hunting

in rat piss

Hope God is coming...

Nothing...,

is what I live for

and can't bring

smiles oh dear lord

I'm turn-ing

into a crack whore

that's fad-ing

into what's no more

The oce-an

feels like the best place

for go-ing

to hide from this race

I'm fro-zen

sittin' at hell's gates

as no one

special to this face

So easily conquered are the unfortunate
with hopes of acceptance and popularity

I knew from the start I never belonged
so the poisoned roots were expected

Green, green grass of home...,

green as shit from an infant child,

lifelong dreams exist in a dope stick

stealing compassion from the heart.

"Does anyone know of my loneliness?"

Urine filled vision of the fuchsia moon,
will any of our names be told in legend?

Faceless, fucked and forgotten,
guilty only in existence

I'm helping none no more,

you're all on my shit list

Venomous villains speaking forgiveness

lead us all to their snake pits

"The birds never sing when I'm awake."

( They only fall to their crushing deaths )

"Who was the first to cry?"


Take me away
from every touch
in the form of a book
they hate so much
to a place
where the mind
is washed when flushed,

remade as a thought
too eager to crush

Take me away
from every dream
on a kite with a soul
and flapping wings
to a moon
with a sun
believed to be,

the start of it all
on the end of a string

Take me away
from every mood
in the form of a roach
in search of food
with a bomb
in a box
I can't defuse,

at war with every
second I lose

Take me away
from every face
on a ship on a trip
to outer space
with the hope
that I find
a happy place,

somewhere unknown to
hours that waste


Two eyes
under the moon
half peeled,
bloodshot…

Two eyes
crying entombed
broke down,
uncleansed…

"What do you see?"

I see waves of graves
all unsaved.

Am I the leader
of this brigade?

No names just stains
hanging from chains

Forever encased
in thirst for the rain

No love for the lonely...,

keep the truth from me

"I'm not feeling you."

Love letters to no one,
written for no reason

I just wanna see
if I still care…,

I just wanna see
if I still have it in me…

No blessings were ever sent this way…

No "I love you's" were ever told to me…

All in remembrance are these scars,

… my past lives …

( Tattooed to cocoons
with nothing growing inside )

How many tears fall
in a single year?

How many frowns sit
behind locked doors?

I'm falling…

Conscience come back to me,
demon retreat…

My head is on
your shoulders


Scars connect… hearts…

My heart… a scar, unconnected

like a dove with no head
that still flies

( Words on a trigger )

Stickers…, all in my hands,

self-crucifixion… dying for nothing…

Jesus…,  I love…

Myself ? … ( Not sure )

A sin to live…

This world… a sin itself

My love… I wish to share so bad…,

but no one wants it

(even in my dreams)

"God…, why do you hate me?"

This day…, has been a lonely one

( as well as the rest )

Each breath… is cursed…

In first, "I'll never be"

( Waiting to die )

My hands…,
sore from praying


Unknown…,

unseen

Just shown through dreams

that come to all the
dirtiest of things

27 halos…,

all on the ground

27 eyeballs…,

poked and ripped out

"Looking right at me."

( Hopeless as they can be )

27 ghost ships
sinking at last

27 tear drops
stuck in the past


Why does it take tragedy
to bring us together,

yet take nothing at all
to tear us apart?

"I will never be whole again…,

there's too much of me missing"

Oh great tree
of never-ending green...,

put us in your roots
and turn us into dreams

"We don't wanna hurt anymore."

Enter the rain...,

cleaner of flesh

Break apart the world
one face at a time
to separate the ashes
engraved in our minds

Deserted…,
faceless in the crowd

"We're almost out of breath God,
please come take us now."

Trampled and vandaled
shameful and painful,
here beats the heart
of an angel

Abandoned…,

missing in the sand

"We almost found a way, God,
but never had a chance."

( Who are we? )

Zeros…

Zeros in the dark

Rewarded…,

with arrows through the heart

Destroying…,
what will never be
that could of,
set our troubles free

We're zeros…

Fishing for a laugh
through voices…,

stuck inside a trap

Unheard of…,

looking for a map

Unnoticed…,

falling to the back

…We're zeros…


Somewhere there's a soul that cares
and shares its wonders
to those that's weak

It calls and cries to all whoever
cast and place
their tears in me

Somewhere there's a dream that's real
to feel and touch
if cared to have

It comes and stays to all whoever
wish for things
to kill what's bad


Pebble tombstones...,

( bones of the earth )

A fucked up virgin...,

my prey

Dream of the warrior
in search of blood

"Are we dead?"

( Only in spirit )

"Now go away!"

I'm in a deep trance
of denial
on the back roads
of life

( stuck in reverse )

Inheriting the power
of the dragon,

( head 7 )

Destroying me every day...,

a smile

( Cataclysmic )

I piss in gloves
to hold hands

( Inner self abomination )

Do you see me?

I'm right the fuck
in front of you

Dissolving...,

lost in an aqua dream

"Who the fuck is yelling?"

( I guess just me )

In need of a concept
never meant to be…

Does God have a fork tongue?


I'm so alone
and so afraid
I'm searching for
an early grave

My strength is gone
my heart is weak

All I can do
is shit and sleep

I'm too broke down
and too far gone

Amongst your eyes
I don't belong

I'm too misused
and dead in need

Fuck this world
it ain't for me

Within your mind
I see my face
up in a race
in dead last place

Trying so hard
to gain some ground
but I can't move…,
I'm not allowed

Your laughter rips
my heart in two
and puts me in
the worst of moods

Disguising all
my feelings blue
I'm nothing good
if good for you

Perfect picture
include me not

I'm just a hole
from bullets shot

I'll never be
what all you need
or all that's left
there in between

I'm just a waste
of cum and space
within a word
that you'll erase

The truth in me
is never seen

I wish just once
that I could be...,

"somebody"


Six million leaves
fell on top of me,

scattering me along with them
as the wind blew

Three million trees
are a part of me,

I hang from them now
as the vines do

In my chest
an axe shaped heart

( My place to be alone )

Walking in the trail of another...

A snake in the grass

Unseen as the days
that pass

I'm here…

bringing up
the rear

Lost in a world
of corners…,

running from infection

I seek the opinion election

"Who am I to love?"

Red dream fraud…,

feel so odd

I don't hear
the voice of God

Maybe I'm a heathen

(drug induced semen)

"I've got a bone to pick."

( My own )

Begging for innocence

Too late…,
it sleeps now
at the wake

(Sleeping on a cross)

I miss the things
I've lost...,

especially my heart

Toying with damnation...

"God…,

is there any soul
worth saving?"


Creating...,

a heart ripped in two

Saved by a dagger

"I still believe in God...,
he's just so hard to see."

Goodbyes voiced over
inside trapped boxes,
forgotten through time
knocked up in a coffin

Running through me like fear

My tears...,
mixing into the rain

"Why should I test the waters
when I already know
they're way too cold?"

(Sanity removed)

"Somewhere in a thorn bush."

No one counts anymore...,

(only their scars)

Stale as a kiss...,

diseased animation

"How far away is nowhere
if I start to walk right now?"


Crying eyes
up in the sun
hoping for
a storm to come

Placed beneath
a plate of dust
hiding all
that's pure to us

Leaking souls
up on a shelf
praying they
don't go to hell

Reaching out
to dirty jars
on a wish
in shooting stars

Grieving tongues
up in a rock
soon to be
an afterthought

Clinging to
a melting door
on a plane
without a floor

Dying words
up in the sand
looking for
a human hand

Out of touch
and overused
binded to
a shrinking fuse...

( leading to the heart )


New pink scar
of creation...

My feelings…,
needing a vacation
from thoughts
calling on the beast,
to guide me

Hope, so far behind me…

(cursing out my name)

As troubles
continuously
come at me
in doubles

Hating the sight
of people

with love…,
no such thing to me

Deceased, failing
glimpse of peace

"Poison of the world."


I'm just a heartbreak
remade as a candle
leaking on all
who are reaching for me…

Creating new life
through hope and soft voices,
hidden by those
we hate secretly

I'm just a loner
in love with a question

Praying for words
that bring answers to me…

Rethinking my ways
as time becomes shorter,

Seeking to hide
what hurts constantly

I'm just a rain cloud
disguised as a person
spitting on all
who are dirty to me…

Defacing the earth
with tears made of acid,

dripping from wounds
that bleed viscously

I'm just a vision
unknown to the spirit

Screaming through all
who are thinking of me…

Avoiding what's real
by living through mirrors

hangin' on walls
with flies listening


Armageddon on stage…,

rehearsing its final scene.

A worldwide panic
is at my finger tips

A worldwide poison
is in my blood

"Nothing will remain untouched."

(Cry no more for the setting of the sun)

"I've heard the voice in the wind."

9,9,9 upside down on a blue and green tombstone
representing the earth
as a black spray painted rose

"Everyone's here but the savior."

( Please hurry )

( Humanity represented )

"We're no longer in this together."

Dust covered dewdrops
blanket the earth
invading our souls
with visions of meltdowns

"Who's next to cry their eyes
right out of their head?"

We're everything
we're not supposed to be.

We're everyone
we so much claim to hate…

( Mating with reflection )

( Private memory evacuation )

"Are there sympathy cards
for loss of sanity?"

"If so…,

give one to God."


The future's made
inside a grave
by those that have
no place to play

Outside the shade
I'm so afraid
to face myself
as well the day

My body hurts
when babies burp

I think because
I'm made of dirt

and without worth

My favorite shirt
is of my dad
cursing my birth


Becoming a tearful goodbye...

the days ahead

Apocalyptic…,

concerned for no one

My shadow…,

beautiful,
yet demonic

Lead me to the throne
I'm destined to rule upon…,

( God of all creatures bearing a six )

The giver of day…,
taker of tomorrow

Trading souls for checkbooks
and hearts for stamps

( Welcome to the change )

Hungry eyes
on empty plates
hoping for
a face to hate
staining chains
of rusted fate,
back in time
a bit too late

"Welcome to today."

"Who wants to be the hero of this story?"

( Tightly tied away )

Lost as life in the morning...,

conceived in the seat of a car


A once often smile
in memories to rot

Tip-toed on the edge
about to fall off

Pretend wells of wishes
with no coins tossed

Here? Forgot.

Alive...but not

"Who will I love tomorrow?"

To fill the rivers
she emptied her heart

( taking me under as well )

*Bloodlines*

To set the sun
she closed her arms

( Expected with me to fail )

The days will fade
to nights that bleed

The secrets kept
will hide between

What's lost foreseen

( I can't let go )

Face down to walk
this earth alone


"Come again?"

All unclear

What am I
doing here?

Thinking of
yesteryear

( when I was a kid )

Playing free

Letting loose

Favorite book?

Mother Goose

Mixing my
socks and shoes

( Proud to be myself )

Then one day
I grew up...

piece of shit
out of luck

Giving less
than a fuck

( Wound upon the earth )

Mommy cries,
daddy yells

In my head...,

ringing bells

Life is like
garbage pails

( Stinking up the day )

Why was I
even born?

Nothing I'm
better for

Just a stain
on the floor

( Life is just a waste )

"Why am I
writing this?"

Maybe I'll
cut my wrists

No one cares
won't be missed

( Not here anyway )


I just wanna cry
and don't care who knows

There goes...,
my minutes
and years
sinking in tears
aligning themselves
with a lifetime
buried in sin

Things I'll never swim in...,

laughter, love

( All of the above )

Wishes on stars...

( baptized )

Angels in cars

Focused on hearts
with no lives
calling for a change

Avoiding old repents

"Heaven sent?"

( Quite doubtful )

New tomorrows...,

things of the past

A private hell

"Compare me to trash."

Extinct of holy grace

( this crowded place )

"Do smiles glow?"

Don't know...,

I've never seen one

Only frowns
with the pain of Christ

Done more wrong
than right

No light
ever shines on me
and if did...,

my eyes
would only bleed

No one thinks I listen
No one thinks I care
No one thinks the breath of day
should fill my lungs with air

No one thinks I'm special
No one thinks I'm here
No one thinks I'm even good enough
to shed a tear


Shadowed forgotten memories...,

blooming thorns of poison...

Lustful fantasies of the unknown

"My bloody dick... unmatched beauty"

( Psychedelic purification )

My eyes are stained with dreams that burn hope
into something I will never have faith in...

Remembered for all
the wrong reasons

Running from happiness...,

going in circles

I know you're all against me

I can see inside your hearts

They're full of grey
and laced with hate

( Dancing in the dark )

None to choose sides with me...

Have I become a cancer?

Deceiving fate,

erasing days

( Making faces damper )

Pouring rain… windows open

"Is this presence an option?"


I'm lost in thoughts,
forget me nots
and all that's born
lives, dies and rots

Paused in shock
and stuck on first

At peace with words
that curse my birth


Let's all fall head first.
"Goodbye!"

Let's all trade our hearts for eyes

Let's all move away from time
and start a world where no one cries

Let's all run and not turn back

Let's all go where no one's at

Let's all dive inside a hat
and find a head on which to nap

Let's all dance and let's all sing

Let's join hands and find our dreams

Let's all hope to be redeemed
so we can live amongst the kings

Let's all leave or let's all stay

Let's all shine or let's all fade

Let's all try and let's all pray

to never blow ourselves away


"The water's so dirty."

( Reminds me of life )

There's a cross on the side
of buzzards...,

picking at the eyes
of crucified warriors

( Brains on a porch )

I saw a river of urine
in a forest of warts

"The hereafter?"

There's chatter,
our time is soon to end

( Days in bones )

Six stones
mark my wasted life

Through a crippled dream
I'm king
of all that's
uncleansed

( Heads in a gutter )

Each other…,
I think we hate
the most

So here's to what
the future holds

as souls
turn into worms…,

raped by sticks and berries

Nestled in a snake's tongue...

sipping bloody marys

"The time for peace is over."

"Come now…,

the fall of man."


As all… my tears… run down…

…all I… can do… is frown…

The light… in me… is gone…

…so much …I do… so wrong…

These days… they are… so dark…

…just as… the hu-… man heart…

No one… needs me… at all…

…nothing… to break… my fall…

So lost… I am… right now…

…To love… I don't… know how…

I wish… the end… would come…

…so I… wouldn't have… to run…,

…no more

Feel better ?

"No."

"I cut myself too deep."

Able to sleep?

"No."

"Too many headless sheep."

( Kinda hard to count them )

4, 5, 6... 6... 6

"I'm stuck on 6."

Wild walks of life,

futuristic kites

T.V.'s in
a cumshot

Robots...,
here after
we rot

America...,

death capitol
of the world

"We kill ourselves the best."

Strength to live
we all need...,

lost in pills
and old dreams

Such things as positives?

"No."

A direction we'll never go...,

...... up.

"Is it possible to love yourself
and hate yourself
all at the same time?"

"It has to be...,

cause that's exactly how I feel
about myself."

( Begging for comfort )

I'm under...,

all that makes
you wonder


Does anyone have a hand to reach out to?
Does anyone have a smile to share?
Does anyone have an answer to give me
for questions on why the fuck I should care
about anything?

It's just a matter of time
till this world becomes nothing more
than a tomb for mankind,
rotting eternally
in the head of sane minds
simmering on the sun

( We have no chances left )

Unstable voice
of dawn's decision,
keep the days moving
through lights made of crystal

"Our tears deserve to sparkle...,

falling next to heaven."

Does anyone have a joy to cry out to?
Does anyone have a tear left to weep?
Has anyone ever lived for a moment
stuck in the secrets of recurring dreams?

…I have…

Ice filled veins
of misplaced creation
create new killers
from the sickness of a frown

"I doubt we'll ever smile again
and why should we?"

It's just a matter of time
till the stars spill from the sky
crushing the earth
to millions of pieces
bursting in our hearts

"We are nearing the end."

( Never more deserving )


In steps I can't retrace
In marks I'll soon erase
In words perceived as fake

I wish you all away

In winds beyond the waves
In tombs beyond the grave
In life unmeant to save

I wish you all away

In sands that seem to paint
In minds I'm sure to taint
In dreams appearing faint

I wish you all away

In time exceeding space
In feelings gone to waste
In love without the taste

I wish you all away


Following a leader led only by the arrogance of himself...

( Walking last in line )

The trail is narrowing...,

instinct on edge holding on to me

"How can I be myself
when I don't know who I am?"

Breath of morning resting comfortably nested
between the earth's pores

"Follow the path of yesterday to eclipse reality"

( Claymation distress comes in packages of three )

"I hate this world."

Papier mâché memories delay the coming...

( Angelic flashes )

"Finally allowed to see the beauty...,

but not ready"

Unsolvable problems…

See through solutions...

( The flaming sword returns )

"Strap on your wings, it's time to fly."

Pass the sky this way… ( moon child )

Inside the platinum patches of layered space...,
salvation is seen but unreachable

( Impersonating myself... God cries again )

Tell me an unwritten story of truth...

Tell me of faith

( Desperate for a hero that will never come )

Inside the dark wish of a shadow's thought
the earth has no choice but to suffer...

It will give what it receives

Enter extinction...,

...the final chapter


Your heart holds nothing
but hate for me
so why do you say
you pray for me?

I'm nothing at all
you claim to be
so how can you say
you relate to me?

What's given is taken
away from me
My face you are
ashamed to see

Nothing I have but
wasted dreams
here in a world
unsafe to me

You live your life
one day at a time
so perfect it seems
compared to mine

Never looking forward,
never looking behind

"How do you hold
your head so high?"

This world through my eyes
you just don't see,
so how would you know
what's best for me?

Unmeant for all
that's meant to be,
nothing I know
is here for me

So how can you say
you relate to me
when I'm all that you'd
hate to be

Swimming through tears
encasing me,
does heaven even hold a
place for me?

This whole world is
raping me
continuously
degrading me

So how can you say
you pray for me
yet curse the very
air I breathe


"Wanna witness a self-destruction?"

Tears erupting,
constantly
up out the eyes
of God

( Secrets of the half moon )

At high noon, this world will
become flat

( Pain of reality )

Immortality,
only…to those holy
1%

"It's normal for things to be shitty"

Gritty… is the taste in my mouth

Taste of the world…,

taste of life

I cried fifteen times
last night…,
…for a reason that's yet
to exist

Shattered
with a demon in my fist…,

punching me all the time

My soul…,
on a thin red line

( Sitting inside a circle )

Headless…,

still moving…

Unattached to the world

"Never was."

A snake…,
freeing itself
of burdens

My brain…,
oh so close to hell

( Home of a future murderer )

My heart…,

beats as though its trapped

Fortress full
of glitter

10 sinners,

live inside my head

( Drenched in dead beliefs )

Hands pressed on
the sun

If only these tears would leave
instead of come

My soul is heavy

In bellies… of beast
we're soon
to be in

Feeding on rotting
locust

Eyes open…,

as the world
around me
closes


Wicked wind,

I play pretend

every time I laugh
or grin

( Run or hide )

Am I alive...,

or inside an eye
that's blind?

Falling rock,

I think I'm locked

up in you
within a knot

Sitting still,
full of pills

Asking if
I'm even real


This story?

( Tragic )

As well as all

I suppose

Without clothes…

The devil…,

his dick in me

The sun,

an ash

disintegrating…,

becoming my brain

( somewhere in the past )

Roads on fire…,

…one ways…

leading straight
to hell.


Demons in the sky
with knives,

disguised
as angels
in troubled times

This earth…,

the suicide
of God

Our hearts…,

a bullet to
the brain


Alone I sit in a world
surrounded by feathers

Awaiting the arrival
of a self-made scar

A beaten one…

Always quick
to beat myself

I'm falling…,

once again
to hell

( Screaming for the birds )

…Wings…

Save me dear lord, please…

*Bloodlines*

I'm broken

Glass in the mirror

My face...,

cracked...

Three crosses
tied to my back

( No savior comes )

even as the tears
of millions run

I question...,

all I won't become

and can't

( Heads on top of shit )

To bits...,

my heart has now
evolved

If I run,

don't chase me…

If I cry,

don't face me…

"I'm liable to break your neck."

( Eyes mist )

Next to wreck?

"My soul."

Close to another meltdown…

…In hell,

everything I am now

( Torn between worlds )

Scattering heads...

My lips…,

two swords,

( Blowing the dicks of demons )

Impossible to love...

( Dipped in salt )

Inventions of newer faults

"Why is a smile so lazy...,

and lately…,

it seems God is
as well

( Whispers behind my back )

There's nowhere left to turn to
but through
a consumed
train of thought

( Burnt )

"I feel like starting a war."

I'm bored…,

and tired of hurting
myself

The trees have wings
in my dreams…

The ocean has eyes…

The clouds have teeth

( The days supply no relief )

I kneel without
knees
to the king of
disease

No more will my heart
( break )

cause I now know
it's me I can't take

Hoping for a fucking earth
quake

One that will
shake us
free from our
faces

Our lives are all
just "can'ts"

No different from worms,
ticks,
leeches
or ants

With the devil we're sure
to dance...,

leading of course

We're all just warts...

unknown to where
we stand

I have nobody…

( My soul is foggy )

A curse upon
this land...,

it seems I may be.

"Someone save me."


A rainbow comes
when I piss myself…

( Visions in violet rain )

I don't get warm days…,

only cold ones

( Bombs in my cock )

In common,
the things we've got…

…nothing

( Same as all )

Phone rings...

"It's no one."

"I pushed the ringer myself."

Outside the sun shines…,

inside… it's dark

Same as the spirit,

bleeding…,

a poisoned mind

( Y'all call it crying )


Falling down…,
feeling down…,

killing off the truth again

Coming down…,
broken down…,

soon to be abused again

Falling down…,
feeling down…,

finding ways to lose again

Pouring down…,
storming down…,

bleeding cause of you again

Falling down…,
feeling down…,

think I've got the flu again

Pouring down…,
storming down…,

tears are on the move again

Falling down…,
feeling down…,

screws becoming loose again

Coming down…,
broken down…,

here I sit so blue again


Freedom of the ants…,

killers of day

Fresh blood…

free of charge

An angel's hug…

extinct in ways
unknown

Home grown,

pain… it hurts so bad

"What show are we on?"

Bad decisions,

I seem to always
make

Don't wanna love yet
don't wanna hate

( A fuck up )

Our hearts were made
to break

Hell over Heaven

This country…,

obsessed with death

( As well the rest of the world )

Three swirls,

each forming a six

Get ready to run like never before,

here comes the fallen' angel

( Dead stars )

Wishes we've never made
create…,

the coming of
end time flames


On plates with bleeding sores
and pus from dirty pores

This snake gave me an apple
laced with bones and gravel

I guess it is religious

( A symbol of forgiveness )

Brains becoming blisters

Brothers fucking sisters

If only little naps
could bring yesterday back…,

I'd see the world better
through any kind of weather

But who am I to kid,
it's hard to even live

on this earth that is
a crack in heaven's ribs


My knees...,

scraped
beyond belief

( I'm lost )

Dreams…,

show me as what I'm not

( A person )

Flirting...,

with tongues made of
bear skulls

Werewolves...,

dance when I'm
suicidal

My heart is leaking out
the corners of my mouth

My face is just a crack
in bones of broken backs

My love's become a fist
through glass and flapping lips

My soul an aching truth
existing without proof

My eyes demonic bells
obsessed with wishing wells

My tears a leaking fate
of me and who I hate

My touch a lava gush
surprised if loved too much

My fall I cannot stop

"God sent?" It seems I'm not


Poison in the rain…,

tears in the poison…

God's tears,

my tears...,

the tears of all

( Fears )

Can babies crawl
in heaven
without legs
and no heads?

( Baited by monsters )

The human mind...,

a nightmare
in the skull


I've drawn the interest
of the peasants

Resentment...,

the day I entered
this world

A tunnel of life?

"No"

( More like a doorway to death )

Blood covered head,
soul…

more of what
the future holds

Unheld…,

was me
in the condom

Open, split
holes
of mother

Bloody grips
surround
each lover

"My nuts on a torch."

( Evil in the form of good )

I'll save you…,

but first I'll have to
break you

The devil's walk...

Same as God's

This world...,

a book
with no
happy ending


Have you've ever experienced deja vu
in a dream?

I have

...removed from a stomach,
...removed form a stomach

Have you've ever experienced deja vu
in a dream?

I have

Here in a new world...,

wanna test saviors?"

Where do I stand
in this journey ahead?

On crutches if favored…,

or food for the dead?

What will I be
in your nightmares tonight?

A version of rape or

the love of your life?

Excluded…,

now on a war path,

my goal to kill all

( Pinch me )

"I'm awake now."

"Time to sing."

*Bloodlines*

People that sit to themselves
are all in my heart
wishing in walls
falling apart,
leaking through shells
lost in the dark

"Why can't I be a winner?"

Sedated...,

back to sleep

Each star is a hole
in the floor of heaven
created by those we've once loved
and have yet
to forget about

Scars in the sky...,

repainted wishes
rc-shown through a mcmory

( Avoided )

*...Enter the flames...*

Welcome to the town
of dead dreams.

Everything you hate
will fill your days
and everyone you love
will die of AIDS.

WAKE UP!!

"Did I scare you?"

( Vacant face of expression )

So what,
if I kill you

( Ruthless thought of aggression )

I swallowed God when I was five
in the form of a cricket,
burning on a plate full
of newborn swastikas.

Salvation's guaranteed
if true to yourself,

but I'm not

So condemn me.

Collapsing every second…,

my value

( Buried in the sand )

When I cum

the wind blows…,

the moon shows
out from the clouds
beyond

Loud sounds

come from
the depths of hell

When I cum,
stars lose light

Bats gain sight

The sky…

becomes a sacred land

My hand…,

gives birth
to feeling

( Unnatural healing )

All your dreams
when I cum

Unfortunate,
black moon…,
when I cum
goes to crescent shape…

The art of semen
on the face
of a wizard

( Color of loss )

Blizzards…,

in the chambers
of hell

When I cum

tails

fall from the claws
of scorpions

Like rain
on a field
of rice...,

all sins washed

Time stops...

I feel important…

a someone

When I cum
mother's cry…

rivers close,
lakes dry

All the love in the world
leaves my dick

When I cum
the earth gets
sick


Boiling up… soon to snap

First on the list of
God's attack...

( me )

[ Scene changes ]

I'm back in pre-school
taking a nap...,
...
soon to be awaken...

( awaiting molestation )

Finger in the ass,
only 4...

"Why do these things happen?"

Ruined without a choice,
chance... hands holding
ants

stung a thousand times

( Rubbing my eyes )

completely beat

Running...,

with glass
in my feet

In love with
a parasite

( Cursed since day 1 )

"Does anyone have a light here?"

"I'm unclear

to all that's around me."


I can count on one hand
how many people I've liked
throughout my life

I've fought
an unwinnable fight

Patience gone…

Right and wrong…

( both the same to me )

Hating everything...

myself included

Diluted…,

my sense to be

"Where do colors come from,

... clouds form?"

My heart's not broke,

its torn

( Pieces uncountable )

Reborn...,

only in fire

"I could give two shits
of your feelings."

This world...,

crooked in its dealings


Flashing colors...

Two rainbows...,

spewing a violet blood

This love…,

dangerous to all
who seek it


Strangers in the womb…,

aborted…

( Hugs and kisses lost )

Goodbye to those
unknown…

Ill doves…,

resting themselves
upon me

So much shame
within me,

I envy…

those that love
their name

( Angels in a knot )

Demons…,

inventors of human thought

Words of a baby…,

crying

I'm dying…,

dead…

Beside me
a head,

looking just like
my mother's

Come green winter

I need you

Pink glitter…,

makes me feel
as the fleas do

( Blood upon my mouth )

I pout…,

whenever people smile

Stuck within
my own cold chills,
for real…

My tears become
a shield...

( guarding my face to all )


Blood on a wishbone...

The unknown…,

my conscience

(spitting out teeth)

In a brand new heartbreak
lies my belief

(sketches of lost hopes)

Uncleansed…

Friends,

see me as shit

Tears on my sleeves...
bombs in my pocket...

The ball...,

I've dropped it

way too many times

Captain of
the cross

The establishment
of zero

( Mind games )

The twisting of
a knot

Everyone's cold...

but I'm not

( Unfortunate )

My soul...

I've tortured it
in so many kinds of ways

"Piece of shit!"

( No better than demons )

You people…

are nothing but
diseases

(spreading through the air)

It's not fair… being
the only one
who cares

End of time…

Hearts and minds

The stairway to heaven…

(impossible to climb)

"All the steps are missing."

Every path I seem to take…,

unwalkable

Steps have now each day become

impossible

Swimming against the waves...

Nothing will ever change...

"Why won't these tears run dry?"

Broken hearts immune to feel

unfixable

In your eyes I seem to be

invisible

Tomorrow's on the run...

at war with everyone...,

"How does this world still turn?"


If I said I had a gun to my head,
would you at least tell me
to pull the trigger?

Master god temptation...

( the birth of the devil )

I gave two cents
to gain what I'm worth…

Two cents…,

all that I'm worth

"There's so many bad people in this world
and I think I know them all."

Me, myself and I

Every bad guy…,

( somewhere in my thoughts )

In need of a new forgiveness…

My gift to you,

four scars

that look like Jesus Christ

( Changing the walks of life )

My purpose…,

waiting for me
to come


Home is where the heart is…,

homeless,

without a heart

Without a stage,

without a part

for anyone
that bleeds,
needs
or grieves

Prayers?

More or less
a wish

We itch…,

covered in ticks

Continuing…,

to ruin hearts

just by

continuing to care

"Why do I?"

( No reply )

"Angry with myself."

Around the sun…,

13 storms that's
sure to come

Infecting…,

whichever direction
we're heading

( Hearts of children lost )

Weeping…,

rotting in a net

"Did Christ stop bleeding yet?"

Not sure…

Those holes are oh
so wide


In the middle of want
there's need

Salt...

the ever growing fault
of birth

I hurt,

I think more now
than ever

( Sorry I was born )

Let's mourn,

the death of
conscience

My involvement
with life
seems quite
likely
not so right

I broke my heart
for your own good
and cursed myself
just so you'd laugh

Everything
I wish to be
now lays soiled
cut in half

Matter? "No."

Wasting time...

Future is
so very dim

Don't feel like
I'm even here

Only known
when times are grim

Destroyed? "Yes."

All my will

May as well go
underground

At least there
I won't be seen

by your eyes
and hateful frowns


Beating in my head...,

war rhythms

Four prisms,

surround me
as the sun

Hooks in me
de-cei-ving,

whichever god
can still see

( anything )


Mirrors on the moon
create sky

A new doom

reflects,

us and the mess
we're all in

This heart is...,

covered by flies
and maggots

I've had it

with everyone
under the sun

Heartless..., people

knowing nothing
but darkness

Lethal,

your tongues
have become

Close to hell fire,

this world

( Close to me )

Tomorrow's pain…,

harder

Fucking me…

all with souls

"In the eyes of hate I'm gold."

( Covered with diamonds )


Shadows bounce from one stop to another
in an everyday rotation

( Concrete creation of the lunar armada )

Sour minds supply candy nature,

rewarded only
in the drop of a tear

"Seeing you laugh puts me on all flat tires."

Ruts fill the fields
of summer love,

leaving the memories
unwashed

( Speaking through heartbeats,

frozen in time )

"Being with you is like making love to fire."

Forgiveness recycled to bullshit…,

non-existent…,

repeating…

"Who's next to fall face first?"


I just want it to rain

…so hard…

so hard I can't see

the world around me

No people,
no pain

If just for a second
it could rain

like never before

Dear Lord…,

please wash
the sadness
away


Flies on shit…

Pricks…,

looking to drip

( Sugar-coated hills )

All the future
on a coin

( Present gone away )

Haven't slept

and soon to wreck

this car I'm in

on purpose.

( Bags around my soul )

My home away
from home...,

Gomorrah

Stones,
crushing all
my bones

"I feel like being missed."

( Needing just to cry )


Vipers...

Insane wanderers...

A sea of sins...

Evil grins
focused

Seems the world's homeless...

On notice...,

hoping to find love

Cold blood

fills it's broken heart

Denying myself
as human

Choosing...,

to evolve into
a shadow

( Hoping for a soul )

Deep holes,

have become my place
of comfort

"If I could move the sun I would...,

right on top of this earth."

2 cents,
I'm worth

and that's with a heart of gold

I can't believe
what we've become,

feel from

and how we've got
so dumb

minded

I'm numb,
pure scum

From God it seems
we run

blinded

I just don't feel alive anymore

To what do we owe self?


Outside…,

it feels like
I'm inside…

some kind of story

in which I'm dead

Nightly...,

I see things
more brightly

The whole world's shining

(cause I'm not there)

It seems that I'm
a "fuck" your saying

A little game
the world is playing

From every tree

some me
is hanging

For the worse
it seems we're changing


Extinction
I think is needed
for peace
to finally be

Here in a hidden thought...,

me...

...twisting in knots

( Closing in on madness )

The sun...,

an insane
holy flame

questioning the ages

Ageless...,

those that's cageless

( Souls within skulls )


Time line receding...

fleeing...

sanity...

tendons torn

I've worn

these clothes for
twenty days straight

( Think I need a break )

Mistakes

I often make

"Does anyone see the light?"

These chains around me,

tight

Your eyes…,

only see
what they want to

Night time

wishes...

I think is all I have

Dear dad,

rest in peace

( Dried beliefs )

My sheets…,

full of restless
sleep

Tears…,

a soul that's bruised
and beat


Look at the road,

dripping

wet paint
on my shoes

What news

does the paper bring today?

66 dead

from a car bomb

5 kids drowned

by their own mom

Babies in the oven

Preteens on the street

( Dick meat )

"This day,

another sad one."

"This paper...,

the same as yesterdays."

( Why is this to be? )

Dear Doctor,

can you prescribe me
a gun?

My troubles...,

a ton

Numb,

my conscience has come
to be

On three…,

they'll be no more
of me

Quicksand catwalk,

sea salt

greets my wounds
like thorns

( The crown of kings )

Who means
anything to this world?

"The Anti-Christ?"

Christmas lights…,

depress me
when they're on.


When rainbows bleed
they think of me

cryin' on my
shirt and sleeves

head inside,
my heart
( I hide )

Praying for relief

When rainbows fade
they become graves

full of words they'd
like to say

cold inside
the tears they hide

"Is this all a play?"

When rainbows piss
they make a wish

upon the stars
we humans miss

hot inside,
the tombs they hide

( biting off their lips )

*Bloodlines*

When rainbows sing
they hope to bring

a smile to those
who feel the sting-
ing hurt inside

( No place to hide )

"A king only in dream."


Do you feel sorry for anyone?

( I think not )

You only care
for yourself

( Product of hell )

Souls for sale…,

99 cents a piece

Release… me,
please…

from your imagination

Christopher Alexander Berg

Space stations,

mix well in
the desert

Recluses…,

moonwalk the best

When the sun sets, I rest
and become a flapping tongue

On the run…

and in search of my
serpent master

I have visions of fire
during orgasm…

Retracting rainbows…,

retracing steps

There's pieces of wire
in my sarcasm

barbed and charged…

277

( hoping to dance )

"This ink's become my blood."

Please hug me now,

a soon meltdown

is coming to
close me shut

Prayer after prayer
in circles,
everywhere

These walls too tall
to tear

Too high to climb

( too tired to try )

This heart...,

too cold
to beat

Baby pictures...

Shooting galleries

Blood splattering…

Iron nails

Church bells…,

get me
spiritually
high

"We've all been crucified."

Hands tied…,

behind my back

Sanity

left at home

becoming bones,

dust…,

shit of the earth

I must…,

get out of here
soon

Dark rooms…,

are all I have
to cling to


In my head
a forward motion

keeping all
what's closing open

screaming out
to be forgiven

but no one
is here to listen

In my head
a backwards message

keeping all
the world guessin'

whose day will I
mess up next?

"I think I just
need some rest."


Cannot connect to server...

Murder…,

it seems is all we're good at

Put back

your heart inside your chest

I stress,

these words now more than ever

"Who's gonna fix the world?"

( Who knows? )

Smiles are just
for show

Full of frauds

and man-made gods

Reality…,

the most distorted

Arousing ...,

beheaded erections

pouting

Brains within veins,

counting

ways to stop believing

Time to take a nap

and dream of
places I'm not at

Hands of fate,

shape and break

Fall, dear leaves
above me

Full of hate,

I can't take

Needing someone
to love me


I fell into ice…

reached for a twig

( I thought was a hand )

it broke

Lying in mud…

hoping for sun

It's raining and now

I'm soaked


I'm lost as a child
lost in the desert

Dead as a feather

part of the never…,

was or will's

I can feel

( when someone's against me )

Test of time
on probation…,

due to crimes
of my creation

It seems my face
leads to motives...

even though
I'm barely noticed


In sure madness, I write this

with a clinched fist
beating against my head

I need to be fed
and blood sounds good

"What's another scar?"

( No one sees me anyway )

Haunting me, a ghost is...

just to feel some closeness

Always been unnoticed

( till shadows came along )

Constantly cut open

Spewing blood in motion

Here I lie as frozen

( grass upon a grave )


I can be your wonder boy,
ready at will to deploy

Head is filled with pointed rocks

( Future in a wooden box )

You can save me if you want
or can use me on your hunt

I don't know, I'm just a kid…,
paying for the things you did

Black is the day, blown away…,

( I'm in the ash now )

Feeling is gone, so is dawn…,

( I'm in the ash now )

Dying for looks, for the crooks…,

( I'm in the ash now )

Born into death, nothing's left…,

( I'm in the ash now )

I can be your wonder god,
part of every growing fraud

In my heart, a ticking bomb
filled with every right and wrong

Please include me for a laugh,
right before I'm blown in half

Tell my wife, I love her dear…

( Here I cry my final tear )

Innocence dead, where's my head?

( I'm in the ash now )

Lying in mud, pissing blood

( I'm in the ash now )

Losing my soul, I'm so cold…,

( I'm in the ash now )

Rotting alone, missing bones…,

( I'm in the ash now )


In hell
we're snails
and salt pours
from the sky

Our hearts…,

bubbles

(soon to burst)

Let's play a game called,

"Who Feels the Worst?"

I will start off…

Fake people

(dull needles)

Two faces

I'm wasting

my time,
my words

So bad
I hurt

Fake roses

Brown noses

Lips flapping,

knives stabbing

me in
my back
wherever
I'm at

I'm shaking
and fading
to nothing

I'm ugly

My tears
give strength
to what
can't think

Disbanding

Still standing

Just barely
still caring

Surprised
I've yet
to blow off
my head


Flavored flowers
on the graves
of super powers

( Smell is sour )

Our brains,
could use a shower

"Minds are filthy."

( Corroded thoughts )

"Dear Lot,

I would love to fuck your daughters."

Incest queens,
sex machines…,

lead me to my comfort


There's no such thing
as friends

In reality,

people are shit
in skin

My mentality,

surrounds itself
in bushes

No cushion

is here to break
my fall


Don't think I'm done trying...

I'm just done crying

I'm tired...

I want to go on,
yet don't

I want to be loved,
but won't

To be or not to be
is me...,

redefining definition

A shit position

seems to be my
birth right

Invisible to
sun light

( Hanging from black thorns )

My form…,

lingers now
in quicksand


The yellow brick road
is covered in red

The wizard
we will not see

His legs are broke,

his head ripped off

He's covered in dirt
and fleas

Don't click your heels
cause we're not real
neither are our
surroundings

It's just a dream
within a glimpse

On us,
the world
is bouncing

So we won't see
the wonderful man
and wonderful things
he does

because, because, because
because
he's overdosed
on drugs

Love is gone
and so is he

"I guess it's time to cry."

Cause here we are
just you and me

with cumshots
in our eyes


System malfunction...

I'm punching...,

everything around me,

corrupted…

Dear God,

I pray for an iron fist


Each day,

more of me goes to nowhere...

becoming nothing
but a string
wrapped around
a lighter

On fire...

hoping for water

or a kiss
from an angel


Pyramids in boots

( pretty in space )

An octagon,

two voices,

no choices

"I think I may be dreaming."

Bleeding…

My will,

I keep on reading

( Feels like I'm dead now )

Somehow…,

I see more clearly
at night

( Maybe I'm nocturnal )

Cold-blooded…

A snake dick
rubbing…,

itself across
the grass

Giving life to
poisonous
noises...,

decaying
the inner self

"I am a wing-tip, frozen..., seeking sun."

Where can I find change?

"I wish to travel
away from this
spiritual battle."

"When will tables turn?"

Each day,

new curse words
I learn

then use towards
myself

( Cruel joke of the world )

Even in dream
I'm seen,

only when needed
to laugh at

My face…,

I often slap at

( Trapped within myself )

Love…,

I think I've never
felt

Outdated,

no longer needed

Beating

myself up
constantly

The loss of me
I don't think
would matter

"Who cares?"

( They'd all say )

"Who's he anyway?"

( No one, I guess )


Weight of the world
weightless...,

In space
I'm shameless

hoping the weather
gets bad

So mad,
I could say goodbye
forever

Inside me,
a lever

that triggers a swinging
pendulum

( One thought )

"Am I here or not?"

Troubled by all…,

unable to walk,
even crawl

My body…, so worn down

Hometown,

sees me as a stranger

A memory is…… nothing involving me……

Re-enactments of dreams… awake in sleep…
deep, within nightmares…

The trees, they stare… at me… Seeing demons…
leafless branches… arms,
roots…snakes…irate…,

me, in search of fire……,

Pray for the prostitutes…

Resorts…… my course…… my doors…… are closing

( Blowing kisses into bullets )

Alerts…… efforts…… my birth... a movement

( Open wishes sliced with knives )

"I'm so sick of separation."


"Why must we always have to take sides?"

Knives in the back hurt
dull
or sharpened

"Who's gonna mummify the sky when it dies?"

Off the fields
of dreams
we're carted.

"May goodness come through my sores."


I've chewed my nails so much they're bleeding

On my heart, a buzzard's feeding

This whole place I feel is peeing

on my face… ( I can't stop screaming )

Faceless hesitation

of a time warped creation...

......

Puffs of smoke, we are…

......

on dying sands of time.

*Bloodlines*

Me and you
live inside a room

with walls
trapped on to
our hearts

Bizarre…,

this whole world
of ours

Here we are
tied up in a car,

no breaks

Headed to the stars
through scars

in this world
of ours

Running trains
run from all the shame
we build

Somewhere in the past
we killed

this grand world
of ours

Drunk as hell
in a wishing well

No coins
thrown from those
above

Just noise

in this world
of ours

Lightning strikes
with all of its might

( Ka-Boom! )

Boxed up
with our thoughts
in tombs

and this world
of ours

Bottoms fall
to nowhere at all

In mud,

laying next
to hope
and love

for this world
of ours

As we sit
here in broken bits
on ships
within ghostly
grips

So pissed
at this world
of ours

Darkened clouds
enter hungry mouths
with spells

hoping there's
no death
or hell

for this world
of ours


Symphonies in my head,
concerts...,

each carrying
a cradle

( Labeled )

Stable...,

condition is what
we're all in

Conditioned... at birth

Petition... your worth

"Somebody has to listen."

( even if arms need twisting )

I've been stuck in the same ride
on the same road
with a traffic light
that refuses to say go
for too long now…

( Heading only South )

Run the red light?

I have...

and just end up
right back
where I started

( Circling Hell )

Heat spells…,

keep me feeling
dizzy

"Miss me?"

( No )

( Why should I? )

End time

reflections
of
skeletons

( Our future selves )

Products...,

up for sale

The value of life?

( Low )

"This is the world now."

Don't blow,

that load of yours
too early

Join me

on the run

Day 1 is what
I'm running from

"When will our end come?"

( Whenever I allow it )

Enter the war drums…

Bang! Bang!


Everyday I feel
I'm gonna die

...Question...

Wondering why I
am still alive

...Betten...

days against the
motherfucken nights

...Sweaten...

in my sleep,
demons in my eyes

...Getten...

nothing but trouble
all the time

...Setten...

up myself to fail,
cannot lie

...Pressen...

God for some signals
in the sky

...Heaven...

never seems willing
to reply

...Testen...

Everyday I feel
I'm in a war

...breaking...

On my knees
crying on the floor

...Save me...

Each time worse
than before

...Faking...

smiles like a
motherfucking whore

...Lately...

the pain seems to
hit me much more

...Hating...

being so goddamn
poor

...Facing...

all they claim I have
in store

...Take me...

to a different time
oh, lord

...Changing...

Everyday I feel
I'm something less

...Asking...

why am I always
so depressed

...Lacking...

answers so it seems
I have to guess

...Tracking...

causes of my
motherfucking stress

...Napping...

gotta get a little
fucking rest

...Happi-
ness only comes
with winning bets

...Stabbing...

holes in my
motherfucking chest

...Trapping...

all that I feel
may be blessed

...Adding...

Everyday it seems
will be my last

...Praying...

that I'm not living
in the past

...Straying...

off to myself,
peeling scabs

...Facing...

all that I am
in a mask

...Blaming...

answers for the questions
that I ask

...Taming...

air that I can't
seem to grasp

...Framing...

souls put on hold
soon to crash

...Raining...

in my head, all the time
I'm trashed

...Staining...

... me


I was in a city. Buildings were falling down.
Chaos was everywhere.
Fire, explosions…, dead people all around.

Nothing could hurt me, though.
I was being guided to whatever safe location was left.

Large falling rocks barely missed me…,
if something blew up, I was at just the right distance from it.

Every safe route to take, I was shown.
I followed without question.

I was eventually led to a large, tall building. In fact,
this building was the only building that had no damage.
Even if something hit it…, it made no impact.

An arrow appeared in front of me pointing up.
I instantly knew to climb even without this arrow's help.
And climb I did.

Things were crashing right next to me.
What appeared to be missiles
were hitting right where I was at.
Other than a loud noise, they had no effect.

When I reached the top I heard gunshots.
I saw a team of soldiers shooting at something
but I could not make it out
due to all of the smoke.

A big blue wave of light then appeared from
whatever it was they were shooting at,
killing them all instantly. After seeing this,
I leaped over the edge of the building
and started to climb back down.

A voice then spoke directly to me within my head.
I was told to come back up top and I did.
Crazy thing is, I was nervous
but not afraid.

When I got back onto the top of the building,
all of the smoke was gone. I was then able to see
what it was the soldiers were firing at.

It was the devil.
This whole time it was the devil.

The devil was guiding me.
The devil saved my life.
The devil was there to greet me.

I didn't know if this was some kind of trick or what
but I was not harmed. No blue wave of light came my way.

Only a smile.

For some reason,
he had love for me.

Genuine love.


Golden eggs...,
babies...

Crazy
backwards world
of ours

Made par...,

drunk and high

Ocean mysteries
within me
exposed...

Thankfully,
gracefully...,

I jump from land
to land

My hands...,

dirty

( hoping to get clean )

Dancing in golden
palaces...

Reality...,
unreal

Salvaging,

what can't burn
in fire

"Hey choir!"

"Chant me a tune."

Leaking...,
hoping...

Hands are open...

Please don't nail
them down.


Snakes and stabbings,

power grabbing

Seems we're all on stage
just acting

out our roles

( Mind controlled )

Doing everything
that we're told


Zero hour…,

zeroed in

Tick, tock

( a mile walk )

The last mile…

Dial ready

Fuse is lit…

Ghost ships,

still in search
of treasure

( Hoping times get better )

Seconds flying…,

minutes dancing

No time for
romancing

"This party's a dull one."

"There's nobody here."


We're all wrong in some ways,

no matter how right we are

We're all dark in shadows,

no matter how bright the stars

We're all lost in some ways,

no matter where on the map

We're all stuck in circles,

running, in and out of traps

Outside there's a demon
singing, calling for my death

Also there's an angel
laughing, placing twisted bets

Inside there's a monster
feeding, peeling skin from dicks

Also there's a wizard
pissing, shitting magic tricks

and so the show begins...

Broken homes equal
broken bones lethal
minds at a young age
trapped in a bird cage

Broken homes bring forth
broken bones reach for
change for the unsaved
heart with no last name

Broken homes shell out
broken bones spell out
words in disguised blood
trying to find love

Broken homes make for
broken bones pray for
ways out of hardships
out on a starship


Sadly,

I'm mistaken
again

My sins

appear to be
a virus

Lifeless,

my movement

( surrounded by serpents )

Nudists on PCP
believing they're
Adam & Eve

All I can offer
is everything

you don't need

Like me

( abandoned )

Demanding,

at least
a good dream

( In need of vacation )

Replacing…,

all the mind's
erasing

*Bloodlines*

My soul is full of
lightning…,
striking
every time I
cry

Pouring inside

( flooding )

A life that I've
muddied

Hidden within
something
that riddles
can't explain

Frozen veins…,

cold blooded

Snakes in pain,
sense nothing…,

when coming to claim
their fame

Gang banged…,

bitches
rule creation

"Welcome to Wonderland."


I've wished upon a million stars,

a million times

( A million scars )

Countless nights and countless tears

have filled my days
throughout the years


Tender trees of gracious heart,
please welcome me within

I bring sticks and stones
to party with
and snakes to hold
my sins

"I can see Earth from here…,

…looks small."

We're all

fiction
in the making

Organized,
coke lines

( warm and hibernating )

I have a place for you,
in no place

recognized
by our eyes

Placed within the true
meanings of our lives

( Captivating crystals )

Like missiles,

the sun will soon burst

In thirst, we walk

talking of life and death

Coming full circle...

Hurdles...,

trials of life

( filling my sight )

This could be the last thing
I ever write

"Better make it good"

Concrete facials...,
jungles...,

My hate's stacked up
in bundles

Bags...,
of painted wealth

A fight is coming...,

and many will not
survive.

Two endings...,

all at once

Separate fonts

Earth, it haunts
Heaven
with ghoulish grins

Stranded in the deep end
of life and filthy faces

Can't wait to start erasing
all I dislike

Judged by all...,

hated by many

Enemies...,

most are
to me

# Other works by
# Christopher Alexander Berg

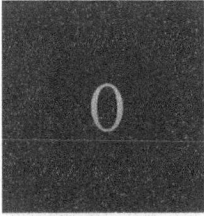

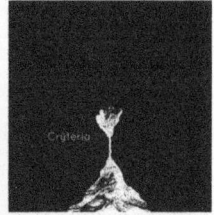

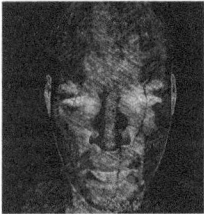

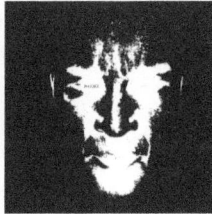

www.ingramcontent.com/pod-product-compliance
Lightning Source LLC
Chambersburg PA
CBHW031234090426
42742CB00007B/196